KABBALAH
DECODER

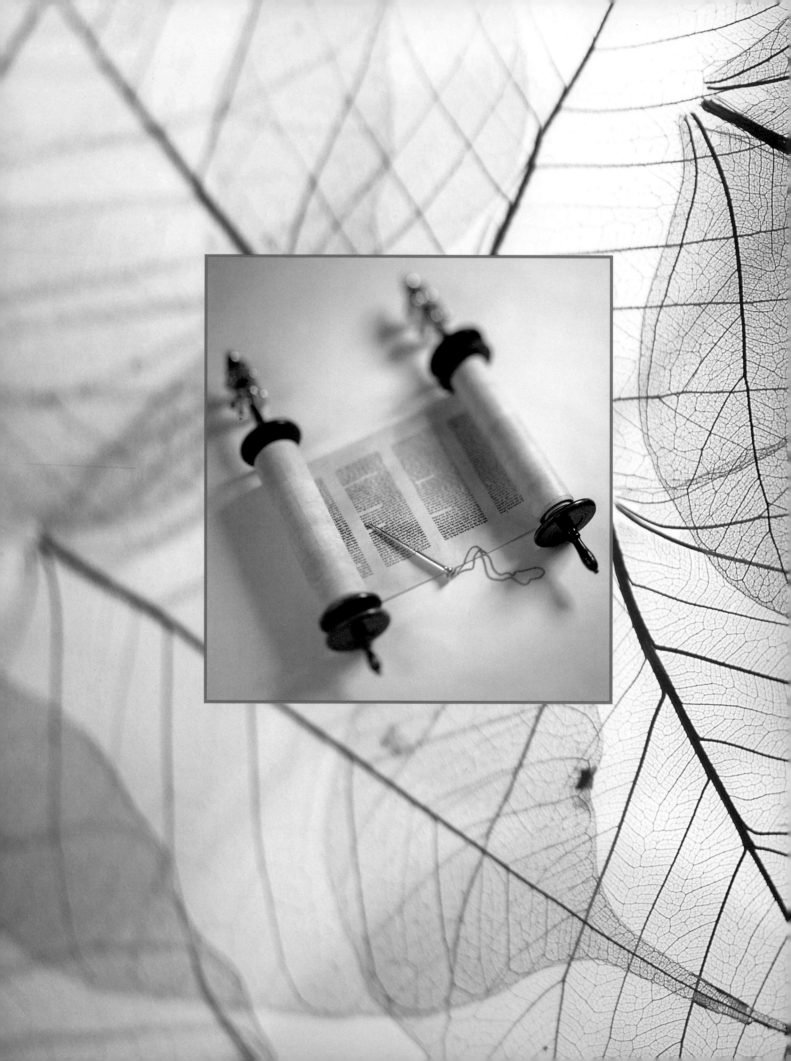

KABBALAH *DECODER*

*Revealing the Messages
of the Ancient Mystics*

JANET BERENSON-PERKINS

BARRON'S

A Quarto Book
Copyright © 2000 Quarto Inc.

First edition for the United States, its territories and dependencies and Canada
Published in 2000 by
Barron's Educational Series, Inc.

All inquiries should be addressed to:
Barron's Educational Series, Inc.
250 Wireless Boulevard
Hauppauge, NY 11788
http://www.barronseduc.com

Library of Congress Cataloging-in-Publication Data

Berenson-Perkins, Janet
    Kabbalah decoder / by Janet Berenson-Perkins.
        p. cm.
    Includes index.
    ISBN 0-7641-5262-9
        1. Cabala_History. I. Title.
    BM526 .B465 2000
    296.1´6_dc21   00-24426

QUAR.KABA

Conceived, designed, and produced by
Quarto Publishing
6 Blundell Street
London N7 9BH

Editor Judith Samuelson
Art Editor Elizabeth Healey
Copy Editor Janet Tabinski
Designer Caroline Grimshaw
Photographer Martin Norris
Illustrators Caroline Grimshaw, Ch'en Ling, Sarah Young
Picture Researcher Laurent Boubounelle
Indexer Dorothy Frame

Art Director Moira Clinch
Publisher Piers Spence

Manufactured by Regent Publishing Services Ltd, China
Printed by Leefung-Asco Printers Limited

9 8 7 6 5 4 3 2 1

CONTENTS

	INTRODUCTION	6
CHAPTER ONE	THE FOUR WORLDS	14
CHAPTER TWO	THE TREE OF LIFE	24
CHAPTER THREE	THE PATHS	56
CHAPTER FOUR	THE POWER OF ANGELS	80
CHAPTER FIVE	MODELS AND MEANINGS	90
CHAPTER SIX	BRINGING KABBALAH INTO YOUR LIFE	110
CHAPTER SEVEN	GREAT MINDS OF KABBALAH	130
	GLOSSARY	140
	INDEX AND CREDITS	142

WHAT *is* KABBALAH?

Kabbalah is the name given to the esoteric mystical move-ment within Judaism, its teachings, and its practices. It comes from the Hebrew root word k-b-l and means "that which is received." Kabbalah is the received wisdom and tradition of mystical knowledge believed to come from God.

▶ GREEN VIOLINIST
This painting by Marc Chagall illustrates the Kabbalistic desire to ascend from the earthly world to higher spiritual realms. Music opens the soul to help this process. The tree and ladder at the base of the picture allude to this desire.

Kabbalah Decoder will introduce you to the major concepts of Kabbalah and the principles and beliefs underlying them. You will learn how to apply the teachings of Kabbalah to your own life as you embark on, or continue with, your per-sonal spiritual journey.

Before you begin, a word of warning is neces-sary. Kabbalah, in all its forms, is an esoteric system that is fundamentally rooted in sincere belief and devotion to God, whatever form that may take for you. Despite its popularity, it is not a fad, a book of divination, or a quick fix, and must be approached with respectful seriousness.

THE BEGINNING OF THE MYSTERY

Tradition has it that the mysteries of Kabbalah were initially revealed by God to the angels, who subsequently transmitted them to human beings, first Adam and then Noah. When God chose Abraham and Sarah to be the parents of the Jewish people, the angels passed on to them this

secret wisdom. One story has it that Abraham recorded the main elements of the teaching in a book, the *Sefer Yetzirah* (Book of Formation), which he hid in a cave. Abraham and Sarah, the first patriarch and matriarch, carried the task of transmitting God's secret teachings to the subse-quent generations, to Isaac and Rebeccah, and through them to Jacob, Rachel, and Leah, and then to Joseph. However, it is said that Joseph died without conveying the knowledge to his chil-dren, and the secret wisdom of God's mysteries was lost until the time of Moses.

▶ TREE OF LIFE
This contemporary version of the Tree of Life is used throughout this book to explain the mystical concepts and inspiration behind Kabbalistic thought.

THE TORAH:

Tree of Life and Source of Wisdom

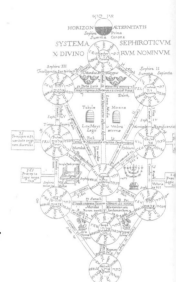

The Torah or "the Law" is the foundation of Jewish teaching, and it is also referred to as "a tree of life to all who hold fast to it." It tells the history of the Creation, and the development of the Jewish people from their nomadic roots, through slavery, to the journey into freedom and peoplehood. Despite its integral connection with the religious and cultural history of the Jews, the Torah offers to any serious seeker of truth insights into the nature of humanity and the soul's search for reunion with the Divine.

▶ TEMPLE PLAN
This seventeenth-century model of the sefirot by Kircher shows the Tree of Life as an overlay of the Temple of Solomon, built almost 3,000 years ago to house the Ark of the Covenant.

From God to the angels;

from the angels to humanity;

from the ancient rabbis to you.

Consider your motives: only pure

hearts and pure minds are invited

to receive these teachings.

OPENING UP THE MYSTERY TODAY

Traditionally, scholars were warned that Kabbalah should only be studied by married men over the age of forty, who were steeped in Jewish knowledge and devoted to religious practice. This ensured that Kabbalah remained an esoteric body of knowledge, not available to either the dabbler or the enthusiast who might be coming from a dishonest position. A story from the *Talmud* indicates the power of mystical knowledge:

Four men entered the Garden, namely Ben Azzai, Ben Zoma, Acher, and Rabbi Akiva. Rabbi Akiva said to them "When we arrive at the stone of pure marble, do not say, 'water, water … '." Ben Azzai looked and died. Of him, Scripture says, "Precious in the sight of the Eternal is the death of His saints" [Psalm 116:14]. Ben Zoma looked and became demented. Of him Scripture says, "Have you found honey? Eat as much as is sufficient for you lest you be filled and vomit it" [Proverbs 25:16]. Acher uprooted the shoots [his confusion caused him to become an apostate]. Rabbi Akiva departed unhurt.

It is said that this story clearly presents the dangers of encountering paradise, or the direct experience of God. Ben Azzai failed because he only applied his intellect. The rabbis say that his desire for God was so great that he gave up his body so that his spirit could remain in paradise. Ben Zoma did not have the strength of mind to deal with what he encountered. Just as too much honey causes vomiting, so he was also overwhelmed. Acher was so confused by the experience that he turned away from Judaism and was thus named Acher, meaning Other, losing his original name, Ben Abuyah. Only Akiva was able to face the experience of the Garden because he was completely integrated spiritually, intellectually, and emotionally.

The restrictions imposed by Kabbalists on studying Kabbalah may have been intended for the individual's protection, but they also closed the book to women, younger students, and anyone who was not part of the small group of scholars.

▲ HOLY SCROLLS
The Torah is seen as a spiritual path and a grounding force to protect the student in search of God.

FIRST STEPS *to* KABBALAH

Before embarking on this journey of the spirit, consider the following fundamental questions:

✡ *Why have you chosen to read this book?*

✡ *Are your motives pure and coming from a place of integrity and honesty?*

✡ *Are you willing and prepared to make changes in your life that may lead you along challenging paths?*

Kabbalah:

Its Sources and Growth

The pre-Kabbalist Jewish mystics based their beliefs on the vision of the Chariot found in Ezekiel. They interpreted the Chariot as a vehicle to enter the heavenly world of God's Throne. Using fasting and repetitions of prayers, they sent their souls upward to penetrate the Throne. For them, this was a form of prayer that let them access the wisdom within the Bible.

▶ Launch Pad
Just as rocket scientists aim for the skies, so the Kabbalists attempt spiritual lift-off in directing their souls through the seven heavenly mansions.

Kabbalah Today

There's no getting away from it—when film stars, singers, and television personalities turn to Kabbalah as a way of finding meaning in their lives, it must be acknowledged that there is something powerful and timeless about Kabbalah that has reached into the minds and hearts of today's materialistic and technocratic society. Wealth, fame, and material success have not brought satisfaction or completeness to people's lives. More and more people are turning to spiritual paths of one form or another. The 1960s and 1970s saw the rise of Western Buddhists, followers of Krishna, and other cults, such as the Maharishi. In the last two decades, perhaps in response to the growing need for spiritual sustenance, more and more movies have addressed the big questions of life, death, reincarnation, and contact with extraterrestrial life.

Religion or Spirituality —or Both?

Membership of conventional religious groups has risen in the United States, and many people have also begun to search for spiritual nourishment in the wisdom of other cultures. Kabbalah is one of these sources of wisdom, but it is also a complete way of life based on prayer, devotion, study, and positive action. Just as Jews flocked to Safed, in Israel, in the fifteenth through seventeenth centuries, so today Jews and non-Jews, believers in God and atheists, scholars and stars are coming to study Kabbalah.

Chabad

The messianic Lubavitch Chasidic movement, Chabad, reaches out to anyone who wishes to return to God, and is gaining adherents all the time. Rabbi Shneur Zalman devised an approach that he based on the higher sefirot of Chokhmah, Binah, and the non-sefirah Da'at, in which students were instructed to meditate on these ineffable spheres of Divine energy. The name "Chabad" is an acronym derived from the names of these three sefirot.

The Kabbalah Center

The Kabbalah Center, originally based in Jerusalem, now with branches in New York, San Francisco, and other cities worldwide, is the

brainchild of Rabbi Yehudah Zvi Brandwein and is currently run by Rabbi Philip S. Berg. It welcomes the followers of all faiths, non-religious people, and anyone seeking spiritual truth and deeper self-understanding.

KABBALAH AND YOU

Whatever has drawn you to the study of Kabbalah, this book offers you a chance to begin to understand some of the concepts and practices. You will need to work hard and sometimes challenge your own comfortable belief system. Although you don't need to be a devout follower of any religion, it is essential to remember that Kabbalah is the product of almost 2,000 years of religious devotion to God. Whatever your religious perspective, as long as you approach this work in a respectful and open-minded way, you can learn from Kabbalah. What you gain from it is up to you. *Kabbalah Decoder* will not attempt to convince you to take

on any specific religious beliefs or practices. Nor does this book endorse or reject any of the schools or organizations mentioned in it.

SEEKING TIMELESS WISDOM

These questions will help you clarify your present spiritual position:

✿ *What do you think you want to learn, and why?*

✿ *What are some of your big spiritual questions?*

✿ *Are you open to the possibility that teachings almost 2,000 years old can speak to you?*

✿ *What does spiritual growth mean to you?*

CHRISTIAN MYSTICS *and* KABBALAH

There are different forms of Kabbalah, which have evolved out of the diverse traditions of the fifteenth through eighteenth centuries in Europe. These variants are a major part of Kabbalah and offer insights into the complex development of Christian theology. Kabbalah Decoder, however, is written from a Jewish standpoint, although its teachings apply to people of any or no religion.

▲ TREE OF JESSE
Based on a tree-like structure, this thirteenth-century French Psalter illustrates the lineal descent from Jesse and David to the Messiah. Saints and angels guard the Tree at every stage.

▶ IN MELANCHOLIA
This image by Albrecht Dürer shows a female figure sitting sadly at the bottom of a ladder contemplating the rock blocking her spiritual ascent. Dürer was almost certainly familiar with Christian Kabbalah that flourished in the sixteenth century.

CHRISTIAN KABBALAH

Christian Kabbalah evolved from two main sources. The first was Jewish converts to Christianity, from the late thirteenth through fifteenth centuries, who composed many texts based on the *Zohar* and other Kabbalistic works. These works were attempts to proselytize and justify a Christian reading of Kabbalistic teachings.

THE RENAISSANCE

The second, more significant source was the Platonic Academy in Florence, established by the patronage of the Medici family during the Renaissance. The founder of the school was Giovanni Pico della Mirandola (1463–1494), known simply as Pico. He and his followers brought to Christian consciousness for the first time a whole body of Jewish theology previously unknown to them. These scholars, steeped in the teachings of Pythagoras and Plato, believed that these ancient teachings could only be understood through a Catholic reading of Kabbalah. In 1486, Pico put forward 900 propositions for public debate in Rome, among which were forty-seven directly from Jewish Kabbalist sources and seventy-two from his own conclusions

about Kabbalah. Another major departure from Jewish Kabbalah was the introduction of Hermetic magic, arising from the Egyptian Hermetic Gnostic movement.

THE REFORMATION

Following Pico, Johannes Reuchlin (1455–1522), a Christian Hebrew scholar, produced two Latin books, *On the Miracle-working Name* and *On the Science of the Kabbalah* (1517). Reuchlin suggested that the diverse names of God revealed three periods of human history. First was the "natural period," characterized by God's revelation to the patriarchs as Shaddai, God of might. Secondly, in the period of the Torah, God communicated to Moses as YHVH, the Tetragrammaton. The third time he called the period of grace, during which the letter *shin*, representing Logos (the word of Christ), was added to the Tetragrammaton to form YHVShH, Yehoshua, or Jesus. Whereas God revealed as YHVH was ineffable and unpronounceable, Jesus represented the coming of an accessible and knowable Deity, whose name could be spoken.

Mystical notions permeated all aspects of culture at this time, a powerful example being the engravings of Albrecht Dürer.

NOTES *on* TRANSLITERATION

✡ There are several variants of transliteration of Hebrew spelling. The following styles are used in this text:

✡ The letters ch, as in the German ich, are used for the Hebrew letter chet, instead of dotted letter h or kh.

✡ The letter k, as in the word keep, is used for the Hebrew letter kaf and kof, instead of q. Q is generally used for the letter kof in scholarly works to distinguish a hard kof from softer kaf. The letter k is used for both sounds in this book.

✡ The letters kh are used for the Hebrew letter chaf.

✡ The letter f is used for the Hebrew letter fay, instead of ph.

✡ tz is used for the Hebrew letter tzadi.

THE RISE OF OCCULT PRACTICES

In Germany, where practical Kabbalah had taken on many superstitious practices, Christian scholars began to synthesize Kabbalistic beliefs with Christian theology. Cornelius Agrippa of Nettesheim wrote *De Occulta Philosophia* in 1531, which led to a widespread association of Christian Kabbalah with numerology and witchcraft. At this time, occult Kabbalah practices began to grow, influenced by and becoming part of the practice of alchemy. One of the greatest of these scholars was Robert Fludd (1574–1637). As interest in practical Kabbalah grew in Europe, Christian fundamentalism reacted against the apparently occult practices, and resulted in witchhunts that killed many thousands of people.

It is noteworthy that the flourishing of Jewish Kabbalah studies in Safed, Israel, had almost no impact on the simultaneous developments that were occurring in Christian Europe at this time.

THE SEVENTEENTH CENTURY

Two scholars encouraged the popularity of Christian Kabbalah in the seventeenth century. Jacob Boehme, whose diagrams form a large part of his writings, helped to make the theoretical notions more accessible. Similarly, Knorr von Rosenroth produced *Kabbalah Denudata* (1677–1684), which opened up esoteric mysticism and incorporated Lurianic ideas.

▲ ST. AUGUSTINE
Carpaccio's St. Augustine personifies the Christian ideal of religious scholar, showing the saint closely studying his astrolabe. God's power was also experienced through the eclipsed sun, which was regarded as a holy sign.

BROADENING YOUR HORIZONS
Recognize the challenge ahead by answering these questions:

✡ To what extent can wisdom from other traditions be integrated with your own philosophy and religious beliefs?

✡ Are you prepared to do the work required to learn about a system of knowledge that may be completely new to you?

✡ How are you a product of your cultural history, and how many of your ideas are a result of your personal searching?

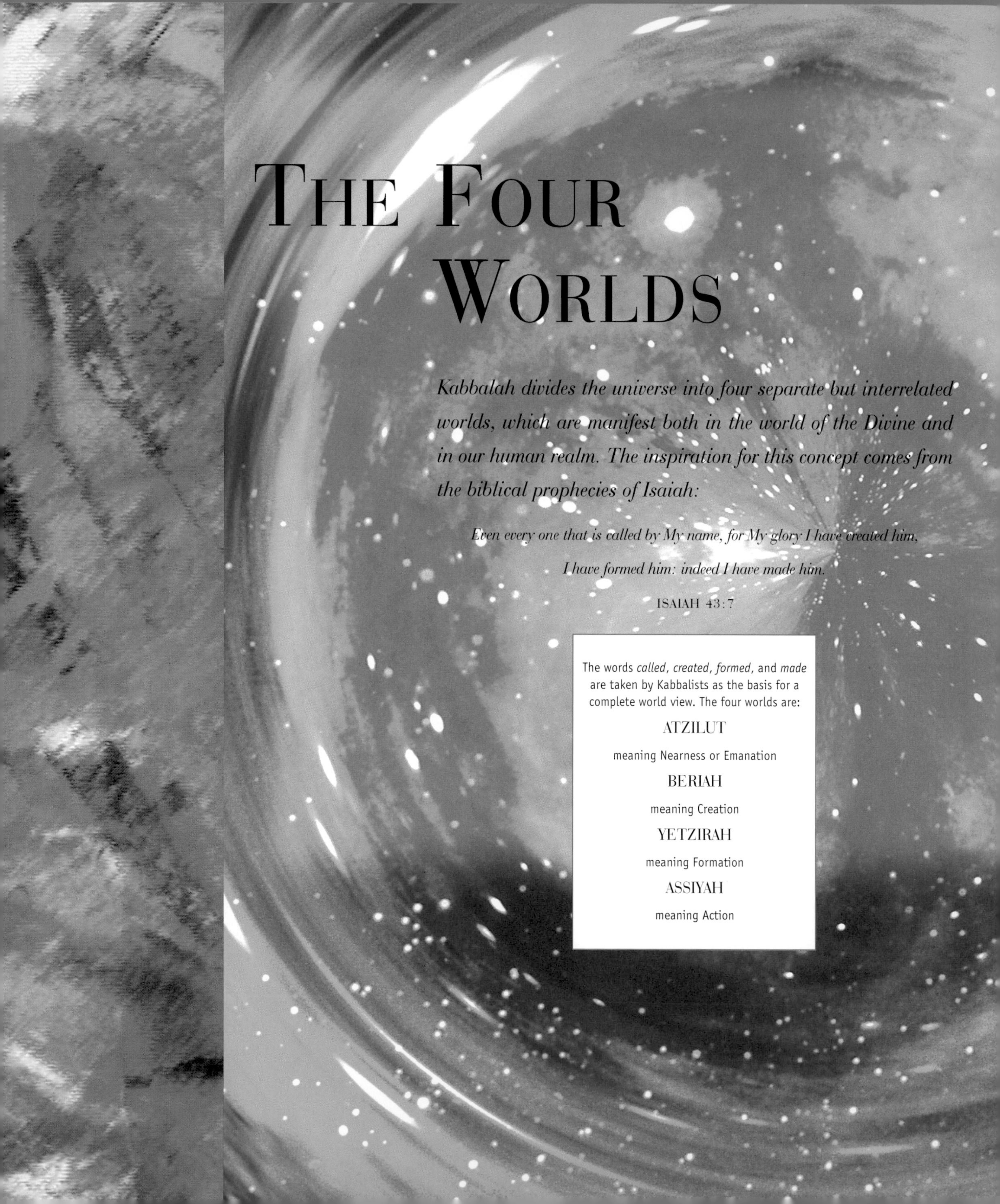

CHAPTER ONE

THE FOUR WORLDS

Kabbalah divides the universe into four separate but interrelated worlds, which are manifest both in the world of the Divine and in our human realm. The inspiration for this concept comes from the biblical prophecies of Isaiah:

Even every one that is called by My name, for My glory I have created him,

I have formed him: indeed I have made him.

ISAIAH 43:7

The words *called*, *created*, *formed*, and *made* are taken by Kabbalists as the basis for a complete world view. The four worlds are:

ATZILUT

meaning Nearness or Emanation

BERIAH

meaning Creation

YETZIRAH

meaning Formation

ASSIYAH

meaning Action

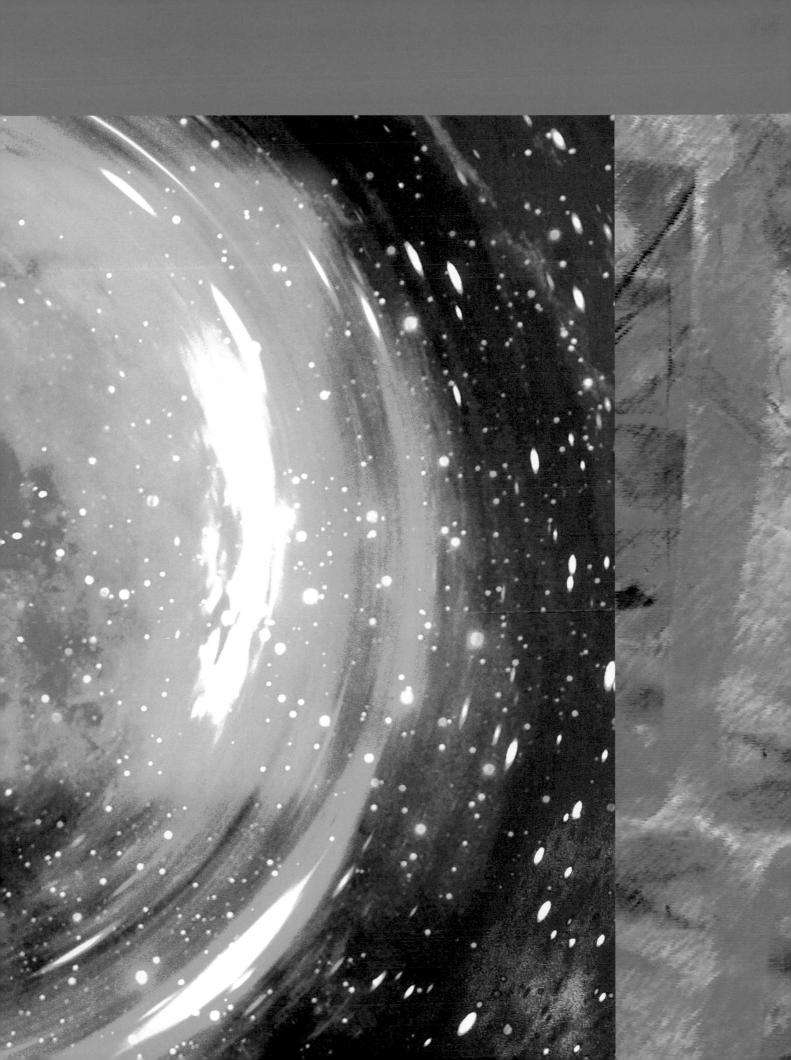

ATZILUT

Nearness, Emanation

אצילות *The world of Atzilut, meaning nearness or emanation, is the highest of the four worlds. It represents the pure and perfect Divine will. It is said that the creation of the universe resulted from the emanation of Divine will, before anything else existed. Tradition also teaches that God spoke ten words that led to Creation, each of these being one of the names and aspects of the Divine.*

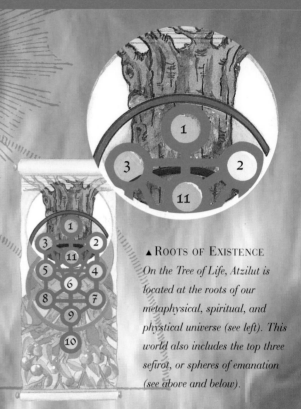

▲ ROOTS OF EXISTENCE
On the Tree of Life, Atzilut is located at the roots of our metaphysical, spiritual, and physical universe (see left). This world also includes the top three sefirot, or spheres of emanation (see above and below).

▲ DIVINE NAME
Each of the four worlds is associated with Divine names for God. This seventeenth century image of the Divine name, YHVH, associates the emanation of Atzilut with the first letter of the word.

THE UNSEEN RADIANCE

Atzilut is associated with the element fire and the realm of spirit; it is the world of God's light, which penetrates and radiates through our world. However, its radiance is often unseen, except by those sages who have dedicated themselves to a life of spiritual awareness and developed an understanding of Divine intention.

Our language and culture have many examples of the recognition that this unseen light exists and can be perceived. We "see the light" at moments of exceptional spiritual revelation; we have a "spark" or "flash" of inspiration; we use a glowing light bulb as a symbol of understanding. Saintly people are spoken of as "radiant with God's light."

NOTHINGNESS AND THE BIG BANG

The realm of Atzilut is linked to Ayn Sof, the Ultimate Nothingness, which was said to exist before the Creation, independent of time and space. The current "big bang" theory also suggests that, before our universe came into being,

SPIRITUAL PARALLELS

As God is known as Ayn Sof, or Nothingness Without End or Beginning, so the Hindu god Brahma is known as Not This, Not That. The three Hindu gods, Brahma, Vishnu, and Krishna, also parallel the three pillars in the world of Atzilut: Brahma is the creative principle, expansive and on the right; Vishnu is the sustaining principle, restrictive and on the left; Krishna is the fulfilling principle positioned in the center.

The concept of kelippot is mirrored in modern virology, which views the virus as an acellular core of nucleic acid in a protein shell. These are thought to be degenerate forms of life, whose nucleic acid has broken away from higher organisms, similar to the kelippot.

place and separated from God. The holy sparks became a reminder of the task that the Kabbalists had to undertake: to try to repair the broken vessels and once again to unify God's light and the dispersed holy sparks. Thus tikkun olam, the repair of the world, remains a task for today: to unify the sparks within us with the Divine will that orders the universe.

Thus Atzilut is the realm of God's glory, which permeates the other three worlds and offers the possibility of coming near to the perfect goodness and light that is the Divine Creator.

▼FIRE
Each of the four worlds is associated with an aspect of Divine energy and one of the four elements. Fire is associated with Atzilut and represents spirit.

everything—the universe—was contracted into a super-dense state of primordial matter that contained all of space and time.

The black hole discovered by astrophysicists may be a physical manifestation of the contraction and nothingness expressed by the idea of Ayn Sof. All matter and energy are sucked into a black hole, which becomes infinitely dense at the center; the gravitational force is so great that even light is unable to escape from it. It cannot be seen, though it can be detected.

CONTRACTION AND EXPANSION

Tzimtzum is the term for the process in which the Divine light contracted, a concept that emerged in the Kabbalistic teachings of Isaac Luria in the sixteenth century. This restriction of the Infinite goodness and light allowed a space for something to come into existence. It also caused the shattering of the vessels that had contained this Divine energy, resulting in the dispersion of holy sparks into the souls of everything that was created. The shells or husks of the vessels, the kelippot, became the material of our world, allowing evil to emerge and fill the spaces. When the vessels containing Divine light burst, everything fell from its proper

The DIVINE INTENTION in YOUR LIFE

Think about whether you align yourself with the Divine emanation by asking yourself these questions:

✡ *What is your will, and what are the motivations underlying it?*

✡ *Do you think that there is an intention underlying the universe?*

✡ *Does your will come from your ego or from the Divine power that orders the universe? How do you tell the difference?*

✡ *Do you ever have a sense that you "see the light?"*

ESSENCE of ATZILUT

Nearness	Light
Inspiration	Nothingness

BERIAH

Creation

בריאה *From the first world of Atzilut (Nearness) emanates the second world, Beriah, the world of creation. Situated on the "trunk" of the Tree of Life, Beriah holds the expansive energy that forms the essential earthly particles of atoms, elements, and stars.*

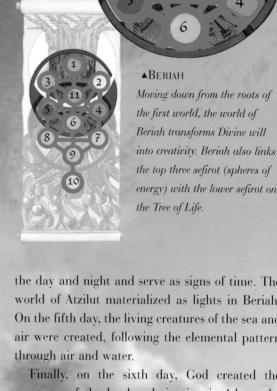

▲ BERIAH
Moving down from the roots of the first world, the world of Beriah transforms Divine will into creativity. Beriah also links the top three sefirot (spheres of energy) with the lower sefirot on the Tree of Life.

The Four Worlds

SEVEN DAYS OF COSMIC ENACTMENT

The seven days, or periods, of creation as described in the Torah are a manifestation of God's will to bring the material world into being. From the pre-existing void came first the creation of light and darkness, which the Divine Spirit saw was good. Next came the expanse, called the heavens, which divided the waters above from those beneath. The world of Beriah governs this second day, and the heavens are filled with archangels who serve the Divine will.

The third day saw the creation of dry land and seas, and the world of Beriah slides into the world of Yetzirah (Formation), in which the creative idea begins to form and take shape. Vegetation, particularly seed-bearing plants, came into being.

On the fourth day, God made lights in the heavens: the sun, moon, and stars to dominate the day and night and serve as signs of time. The world of Atzilut materialized as lights in Beriah. On the fifth day, the living creatures of the sea and air were created, following the elemental pattern through air and water.

Finally, on the sixth day, God created the creatures of the land, culminating in Adam, the human being, and bringing the perfect idea of the world of Beriah into the tangible world of Yetzirah, Formation. When the whole had been created, God saw the interplay and balance between form and function, expansion and contraction, and called the work "very good." On the seventh day, God withdrew from the outward act of creating and rested, bringing into being the concept of rest and Shabbat, the Sabbath.

BERIAH AND THE INTELLECT

The world of Beriah parallels the intellect, the capacity to create an idea and to make it real. But with the intellect comes the appearance of evil. For humanity does not have the inherent balance and totality of God, and personal will finds a path for itself separate from the Divine will. Humans have free will, and therefore also create evil. From this belief arose the notion of reward and punishment. Kabbalah sees this human capacity for thought and creativity as part of the task of being an expression of Divine will. To do this requires a

▼ ADAM AND EVE
Adam and Eve take the first steps towards knowledge in the Garden of Eden.

state of constant consciousness. The study of the Torah and the mystical works of the Kabbalists leads to this heightened state of awareness.

FOUR ELEMENTS OF CREATIVE FORM

Each of the four worlds corresponds to an element: Atzilut, fire; Beriah, air; Yetzirah, water; and Assiyah, earth. Just as Earth developed from its initial fiery gaseous state, cooling to liquid and then solid form, so Kabbalah envisages both the Divine and the human worlds as reflections of this transformation of states of being.

The *Sefer Yetzirah* (Book of Formation) speaks of the elements as follows:

Three mothers … in the Universe are air, water, fire

Heaven was created from fire

Earth was created from water

And air from Breath decides between them.

SEFER YETZIRAH 3:4

▲ GOD AND COMPASSES
In Beriah, the intellect transforms inspiration into creative thought. In this picture by William Blake, God uses a compass to bring creative design into reality.

CREATING *and* REALIZING YOUR IDEAS

Examine the way you use your mind by answering these questions:

✡ *Have you allowed your intellect to flower and develop its potential?*

✡ *To what ends do you exercise the power of your mind and intellect?*

✡ *Are your ideas born out of the selfish will of your ego, or do they reflect an awareness of the universal need for balance and repair?*

✡ *Does your creativity enhance your spiritual life and the lives of those around you?*

✡ *What steps can you take to develop daily consciousness of the right path to walk?*

ESSENCE *of* BERIAH

Awareness	Understanding
Creativity	Pure spirit

The Four Worlds

YETZIRAH

Formation

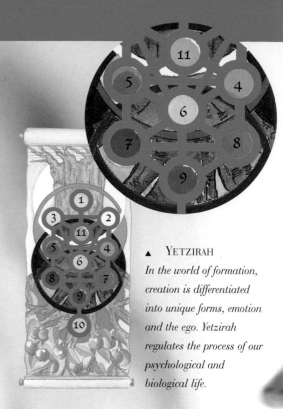

יצירה *Yetzirah describes a continual process of change. In the book of Genesis, Adam is the generic word for the first human and is described as both male and female (hermaphrodite). Later in the story, Adam is transformed into separate male and female beings, whereby Eve is created from his rib as his partner. Yetzirah expresses this differentiation.*

▲ YETZIRAH
In the world of formation, creation is differentiated into unique forms, emotion and the ego. Yetzirah regulates the process of our psychological and biological life.

BRIDGE BETWEEN WORLDS

Whereas the world of Beriah (Creation) is inhabited primarily by archangels, the world of Yetzirah (Formation) is the realm of angels where differentiation and individuation occur. Charles Darwin's observations of finches and other creatures in the Galapagos Islands led him to expound the theory of evolution, in which the variant forms within species develop over time according to the principle of "survival of the fittest" and mutation. Differentiation occurs in Yetzirah, with the angels developing their own individualism in both nature and role. The nineteenth-century concern with form, structure, and function was exemplified by Darwin, who observed that the clear differentiation of animal species took place over time.

Beriah, the world of Intellect, focuses on understanding and wisdom, whereas Yetzirah, the realm of emotion, encompasses the balance between strength and mercy and the expression of beauty. In the Kabbalistic world, strength and mercy, mediated by beauty, and reverberation and eternity, mediated by foundation, govern the forms and interrelationships of life on Earth. The angels, each with a different name and purpose, mediate between the upper world and the lower to facilitate the work that must take place in the world of Assiyah (Action).

YETZIRAH AND THE EMOTIONS

The emotional life of the ego and psychological consciousness exist in the world of Yetzirah. Human beings have both the capacity and the responsibility to develop their awareness of the relationship between body, emotion, intellect, and spirit. Although today the heart is seen as the seat of the emotions, many ancient traditions, including Kabbalah, viewed the heart as the center of knowledge. Even today, we often say "I know it in my heart" to express an understanding beyond reason.

As Aryeh Kaplan explains in his translation and commentary on the *Sefer Yetzirah*, the heart is "king over the soul" (6:3). The word *lev* (spelled in Hebrew *lamed-vet*), which means heart, also stands for the number thirty-two, which represents the thirty-two paths of wisdom, the way to climb to the spiritual realm.

▲ GARDEN OF EDEN
Adam and Eve began their existence in Paradise in a state of innocence that allowed them to interact with God and the angels, but they exercised their will contrary to God and then became responsible for their actions.

SPIRITUAL PARALLELS

The Greek philosopher Plato (ca. 427–347 B.C.E.) believed that the material world is an imperfect copy of the ideal, which exists in a perfect eternal world. Platonic love arises from the best qualities of a person and inspires their development, showing clear similarities with the principles of Yetzirah.

Furthermore, the Torah begins with the letter *vet* and ends with the letter *lamed*. As it is read cyclically every year, the two come together to form the word *lev*, reminding us that the Torah is the heart of God's teaching.

▲ PROGRESS OF LIFE

As seeds germinate, they develop roots and stems. The phototropic (growing toward the light) and geotropic (growing toward the Earth) responses of the cells are an example of differentiation within Yetzirah that is manifested later in the world of Assiyah.

The PART PLAYED by YOUR EMOTIONS

To learn whether your emotions are in balance with the rest of your personality, answer these questions:

✡ *Do you respond or react emotionally to the events of your life?*

✡ *What feelings and thoughts guide your speech?*

✡ *Do you allow the wisdom of your heart to be heard?*

✡ *Does the form of your life—your home, your work, your body, your relationships—reflect your understanding of the balance between judgment/power on the one hand and mercy/love on the other?*

ESSENCE of YETZIRAH

Emotion	Speech
Differentiation	Form

ASSIYAH

Action

The world of Assiyah encompasses action and the realm of the body. This is the earthly world we know, peopled by human beings and animals interacting with plant life and the inorganic world. The upper worlds reach down and interact with the realm of Assiyah (Action) so that what arises from inspiration, creation, and formation can be completed. Assiyah is therefore linked to the concept of completion.

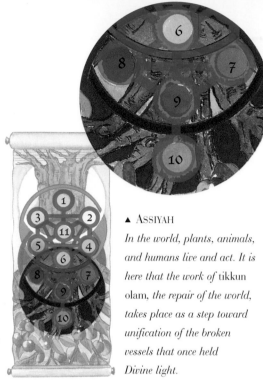

▲ ASSIYAH
In the world, plants, animals, and humans live and act. It is here that the work of tikkun olam, *the repair of the world, takes place as a step toward unification of the broken vessels that once held Divine light.*

▶ MANUAL WORK
This medieval woodcut can be viewed as an example of life in Assiyah—people do the work and toil that is necessary for sustenance. A sovereign figure oversees the events, representing the hierarchy within the sefirah of Malkhut (see pages 52–53).

▶ HOLY HANDS
Two hands outstretched to form the priestly blessing represent a Kabbalistic unification of the four letters that denote the name of God, YHVH.

ASSIYAH AND THE WORLD OF NATURE

In Assiyah, the chemical elements created in Yetzirah combine into animal, vegetable, and mineral existence. Plant and animal cells function according to the principle of "as above, so below." There is a correspondence between the processes of the lower world of Assiyah and the energies of Yetzirah, Beriah, and Atzilut (Formation, Creation, and Nearness).

DNA, the complex molecule that contains everything cells need to make proteins, can be seen as a physical expression of the Tree of Life (see page 30). Each column of nucleotides pairs up in a sequence that carries the genetic code of the organism. The bases link with each other through horizontal bonds, and the whole structure wraps into a double helix. Comparison with the Kabbalistic Tree of Life shows a similarity between scientific and metaphysical reality.

ASPECTS OF THE DIVINE IN ASSIYAH

The sefirot that dominate the world of Assiyah are Hod (Splendor or Reverberation) and Netzach (Victory and Eternity). These are mediated by Yesod (Foundation) and linked to the upper worlds through the energy of Tiferet (Beauty). The daily life and work of the world take place in the sefirah of Malkhut (Kingdom). The energy that descends from the higher sefirot finds expression in the earthly realm.

Jewish tradition teaches that humans are made "in the image of God." This does not mean a physical likeness; rather, it reminds us that in each person is a holy spark that is a part of God, and that our nature reflects and resonates with God's

goodness. It is through the balanced interaction of body, emotions, mind, and spirit that we express our Divine potential.

THE PATH TO UNIFICATION

"It is not your duty to complete the work, but neither are you free to desist from it." This teaching comes from Rabbi Tarfon, a sage from the second century, long before the emergence of Kabbalah as a branch of Jewish study. He was known to favor performance of commandments above study, and his comments presage the Kabbalistic notion that action in the world of Assiyah is the path to unification with God. Each task that we do can be an opportunity to engage in the work of repair and unification. We have no idea of the ramifications of our actions: One good deed may tip the balance of the scales for the whole world.

▼ SCIENCE OF NATURE
The geometric form of crystals is another example of the wonder of creation, as each one is unique and an example of specific molecular structures.

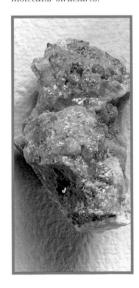

EXPRESSING YOUR DIVINE POTENTIAL

Consider these questions to discover whether your body, emotions, mind, and spirit cooperate with God:

✡ *How often in your daily actions do you consider the consequences of what you do?*

✡ *Do you recognize what work needs to be done, but desist from doing it?*

✡ *How can you inspire your actions and relationships to reflect the goal of unification and repair?*

✡ *Do you acknowledge the holy nature of your body and respect and care for it?*

ESSENCE *of* ASSIYAH

Body	Nature
Work	Repair

CHAPTER TWO

THE TREE OF LIFE

Kabbalah explains reality with a map called the Tree of Life. It stems from twelfth-century Spain—and possibly earlier—when Kabbalists created Sefer ha-Bahir, the Book of Brilliance, *a vision of the universe that both underlies and governs our visible world. For them, the Tree of Life became the central construct to explain everything.*

The Tree is composed of the ten sefirot, which are spheres of Divine attributes. These are

1 KETER

meaning Crown

2 CHOKHMAH

meaning Wisdom

3 BINAH

meaning Understanding

4 CHESED

meaning Mercy

5 GEVURAH

meaning Judgment or Power

6 TIFERET

meaning Beauty

7 NETZACH

meaning Endurance

8 HOD

meaning Glory

9 YESOD

meaning Foundation

10 MALKHUT

meaning Kingdom

WHAT *is the* TREE *of* LIFE?

In Genesis 2:9, we are told that in the Garden of Eden God caused to grow every tree that was pleasing to the sight and good to eat, including the Tree of Life and the Tree of Knowledge of Good and Evil. The Tree of Life, the source of immortality and God's radiance, was given to humanity.

▶ THEORY OF EMANATION
This 1708 illustration is based on Luria's theory of emanation. According to Luria, evil emerged from God, when the vessels holding the Divine light shattered, and the kelippot (shells) were dispersed into the lower world to form Creation.

Early Kabbalists were inspired by the image of this Tree of Life and likened the Torah itself to a tree. The Tree is composed of the ten sefirot: spheres of Divine attributes. These attributes are linked to the word *sappir*, Hebrew for *sapphire*, which indicates the brilliance radiating from God.

THE TREE THAT CONTAINS ALL

The cosmic Tree is seen as the source of life—from the Crown (Keter) that forms the roots from which everything emanates, down through the central pillar or trunk of Knowledge (Da'at), Beauty (Tiferet), Foundation (Yesod), to the branches of the Kingdom (Malkhut). The right and left pillars represent a range of qualities in dynamic opposition and equilibrium. Facing the tree, these qualities align under the pillars as shown below:

LEFT PILLAR	RIGHT PILLAR
Feminine (passive) Principles	Masculine (active) Principles
Eve	Adam
Dark	Light
Written law	Oral law
Discipline	Love
Theory	Practice
Rational intellect	Intuitive wisdom
Judgment	Mercy

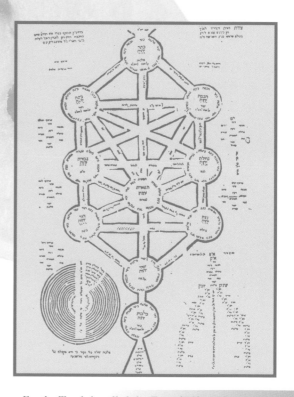

For the Torah is called the Tree of Life … Just as a tree consists of branches and leaves, bark, sap, and roots, each one of which components can be termed tree, … you will also find that the Torah contains many inner and outward things, and all form a single Torah and a tree, without difference between them …

MOSES DE LEON
SEFER HA-RIMMON

Each of these pairs of qualities shown by the pillars of the Tree of Life is governed by the sefirot, all ten of which (plus the eleventh, non-sefirah Da'at) comprise the attributes of the Divine and the system that underlies all life.

LURIA'S TREE

Over the centuries many versions of the Tree of Life have been formulated. The most prominent of these is the system put forward by Rabbi Isaac Luria, known as the Lion (Ari). He lived in sixteenth-century Palestine and studied and taught in the town of Safed, the center of Jewish mysticism, Kabbalah study, and practice.

The Lurianic Tree of Life was devised as a practical application of mystical knowledge in the fight against evil and in the service of Divine intention. Not only was the Tree a description of the structure and nature of the universe, but it also demonstrated a path to bring back righteousness to a society that was considered out of balance, particularly after the experience of the expulsion of the Jews from Spain in 1492.

◄ SYMBOL OF THE FALL
While the apple is a key Christian image in the story of the Creation, Kabbalists take their inspiration from the positive image of the Tree of Life.

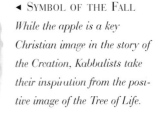

◄ NEW KNOWLEDGE
The Tree of Knowledge of Good and Evil was the only source of food forbidden to Adam and Eve. By eating the fruit from this tree, they became aware of their nakedness and had to take responsibility for their actions.

The ROUTE *to* RIGHTEOUSNESS

You can use the Tree of Life to examine your own sense of equilibrium. Ask yourself these questions as a starting point.

✿ *Do you allow both your masculine and feminine qualities to manifest in your life?*

✿ *Do you have balance in your relationships or do you swing wildly from one extreme to another?*

✿ *How can you begin to create dynamic equilibrium in the actions you take every day?*

ESSENCE *of the* TREE
Active
Passive

FROM *the* COSMOS *to the* SOUL

Jewish oral tradition suggests that in the beginning God taught the secrets of Kabbalah to the angels. It is believed that the angels taught Kabbalah wisdom to humanity to offer people a way back to God after the Fall in Eden. This secret knowledge was passed to Noah, Abraham, and Moses, who then passed it on, along with the Torah, through Joshua to the elders of the Great Assembly.

▶ **TABLETS OF STONE**
When Moses ascended Mount Sinai, there was thunder and lightning and the Earth shook. He descended with the tablets of the Law engraved by God. It is said that the whole of God's teaching was given, complete and perfect, to Moses at that time.

THE THREE PILLARS

One of the last survivors of the Great Assembly, Simon the Just, said:

> *The world stands on three things:*
>
> *on Torah,*
>
> *on service, or prayer*
>
> *on deeds of loving-kindness.*

SAYINGS OF THE FATHERS

These pillars of Judaism are reflected later through the Kabbalistic process of work of unification through contemplation, devotion, and action.

THE KABBALISTS DEVELOP THE TREE

The Tree of Life is not mentioned explicitly in the early Kabbalistic work, the *Sefer Yetzirah*. However, the later works of *Sefer ha-Bahir* and the *Zohar* clearly describe the sefirot:

> *All the divine powers form a succession of layers, and are like a tree.*

SEFER HA-BAHIR

> *Now the Tree of Life extends from above downward, and is the Sun which illuminates all.*

ZOHAR

Thus the Tree of Life becomes the archetypal form to describe the movement of Divine inspiration, wisdom, and energy from above to below, and the simultaneous aspirations of humanity to climb to the realm of God.

THE TEN COMMANDMENTS

The Tree was also used to describe the giving of the Ten Commandments. The Kabbalists saw the Ten Commandments as prescribing a mode of thought, devotion, and action. Each one was seen as an expression of one of the sefirot.

RELATING TO THE DIVINE

The first three commandments prescribe people's relationship to God and the link to the spiritual

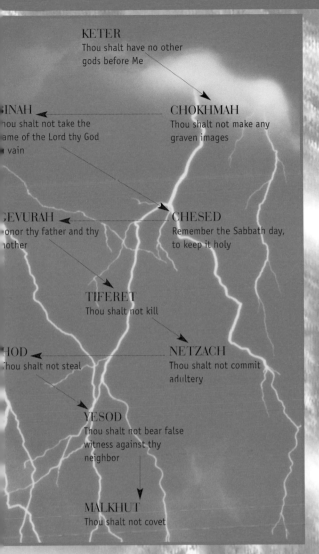

KETER
Thou shalt have no other gods before Me

BINAH
Thou shalt not take the name of the Lord thy God in vain

CHOKHMAH
Thou shalt not make any graven images

GEVURAH
Honor thy father and thy mother

CHESED
Remember the Sabbath day, to keep it holy

TIFERET
Thou shalt not kill

HOD
Thou shalt not steal

NETZACH
Thou shalt not commit adultery

YESOD
Thou shalt not bear false witness against thy neighbor

MALKHUT
Thou shalt not covet

◄ LIGHTNING FLASH
Divine will emanates through the Tree of Life like a flash of lightning, with each sefirah being linked to one of the Ten Commandments.

SPIRITUAL PARALLELS

In Buddhist architecture, the stupa and pagoda express the Tree as the central axis of the universe; each level represents a plane of existence that practitioners aspire to transcend.

of the Sabbath with the formation of the world and God's rest from creating. The Fifth Commandment prescribes the emotional relationship between people and their parents; respect and honor bring long life, because they express the relationship between humanity (the children) and God (the parent).

HUMAN BEHAVIOR AND GOD'S WILL

Commandments Six through Ten, all prohibitions, describe the challenging world of Assiyah (Action). A human being, made in the image of God, must live and demonstrate Divine attributes in action. This is the earthly level, where temptation can overwhelm the knowledge of right action.

world of Atzilut and the intellectual world of Beriah. The First Commandment clarifies God as an expression of perfect unity. The Second Commandment prohibits anything from coming between humanity and God; graven images are prohibited to prevent people from straying into a misguided understanding of the Deity. The worship of success, money, holiness, or beauty are all classed as idolatry. The Third Commandment establishes the connection between speech and an awareness of God's holiness. To swear using God's name is to betray the special relationship with the Divine.

RELATING TO HUMANITY

The Fourth Commandment moves into the world of Yetzirah, linking the remembrance and keeping

LIVING *in the* DIVINE DIMENSION

Answer these questions to clarify the basis for your actions:

✡ *What are the pillars on which your world rests?*

✡ *How do you formulate your rules of right thought and action?*

✡ *How can you integrate the Kabbalistic understanding of the Ten Commandments into your daily thoughts and actions?*

ESSENCE *of* UNIFICATION

Contemplation	Devotion
Rules for taking the right action	

THE TREE of LIFE TODAY

Although the Tree of Life was developed over six hundred years ago, its structure and function are still relevant today. As our knowledge of our world, mind, and body increases, we learn that many early Kabbalistic notions are mirrored in today's science, philosophy, and psychology.

DREAM PSYCHOLOGY

C.G. Jung brought a spiritual dimension to the interpretation of dreams and symbols. He saw them as expressions of archetypes, primordial images from the "collective unconscious" of humanity. For Jung, the Tree of Life represented the transpersonal self, which unites the conscious and unconscious mind and symbolizes the potential completeness of being.

The sefirot are also seen to govern different aspects of being: physiological, emotional, and psychological. Two interconnected trees can demonstrate how all the human processes operate in keeping with the structure of the Tree of Life.

Your brain, spine, genitals, and feet align along the central pillar or trunk, overseen by Keter, Da'at, Tiferet, Yesod, and Malkhut. Your left side is governed by Binah, Gevurah, and Hod, and your right side is directed by Chokhmah, Chesed, and Netzach.

THE EFFECT OF IMBALANCE

Imbalance between the pairs or triads may manifest itself in dysfunction on both physical and psychological levels. The healthy functioning of the nervous and endocrine systems and the organs depends on maintaining a balance between the lower and middle triads. For example, a person who tends toward judgment and the exercise of power, as opposed to mercy and sharing love, may suffer disturbances in his or her metabolism and hormones. On a psychological

level, dependence on the rational intellect at the expense of intuition and spiritual understanding may result in an inability to share emotionally with others and to express feelings. The "head in the clouds" intuitive person, who ignores the importance of learning and reason, may suffer from emotional outbursts and be unable to receive love offered by others.

DNA AND THE TREE OF LIFE

The discovery in 1962 of the molecular structure of DNA by Francis Crick, James Watson, and Maurice Wilkins enabled the world to understand the transmission of genetic material from one generation to another. The huge molecular models that they built have since been seen, identified, and analyzed to show how all the inherited characteristics of an organism are determined and transmitted. The understanding of DNA is now so advanced that biologists have been able to clone organisms and to recombine DNA material to create genetically modified species.

If the double helix structure of DNA is compared to, or superimposed on, the Tree of Life, it becomes possible to see the striking parallel between them. The central pillar of the DNA molecule forms the trunk encircled by the two sugar and phosphate strands. These form the ladder on which the pairs of bases combine to make the rungs. There are sixty-four ways of ordering the combinations of the four bases in groups of three, to create the twenty amino acids

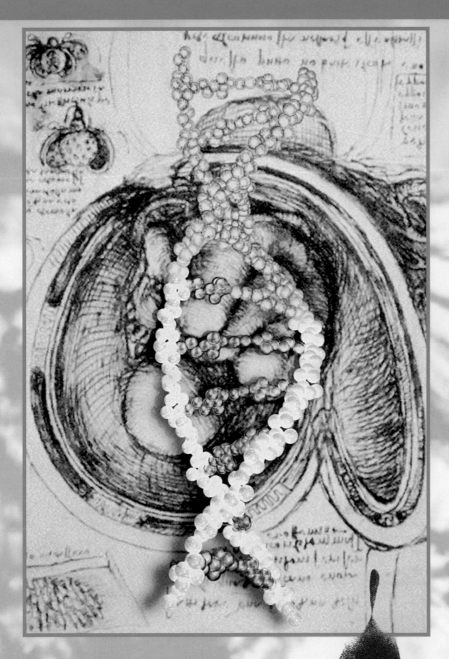

◄ MICROSCOPIC TREE
The DNA double helix structure forms the ladder on which the pairs of bases combine to make the rungs. This unchanging pattern is comparable to the strict order governing the Tree of Life.

FINDING *the* PATH *to* COMPLETENESS

Let these questions guide you as you search for your own approach to spirituality:

✡ *Consider the Tree as a symbol in your life. What images does it bring to mind?*

✡ *Think about your physical and emotional state. How might a daily awareness of the Tree of Life and your body aid in maintaining or recovering health?*

✡ *What paths or connections seem to recur in your life, and what might they indicate about the direction you need to take?*

that compose proteins. Compare this to the twenty-two letters of the Hebrew alphabet and the 231 possible combinations, known as the 231 gates, and the ten sefirot, which combine to create thirty-two paths. Together these paths and gates represent a structured basis of spiritual life and an approach to enlightenment.

► PRIMORDIAL MAN
Kabbalists superimposed the Tree of Life onto the body of the primordial human being who was said to be created in the image of God.

ESSENCE *of* EQUILIBRIUM

Symbols	Balance
Connections	Health

THE SEFIROT

The Tree of Life has ten primary focus points, known as sefirot, or spheres of Divine attributes or energy. Referred to as "the ten sefirot of Nothingness," they are interpreted as "without anything," indicating that they are idealized spiritual concepts with no physical nature. Despite their metaphysical characteristics, the sefirot relate to all aspects of reality and human experience.

The sefirot are introduced at the very beginning of the *Sefer Yetzirah*, the first Kabbalistic text. They are closely associated with the Hebrew words *mispar*, meaning *counting*; *sefer*, meaning *book*; and *sippur*, meaning *communication*. The related word *sappir*, meaning *sapphire*, indicates the radiant power of the sefirot.

NAMES OF THE DIVINE

The ancient rabbis developed many names for God, the one Divine spirit that created and rules the world. The most familiar of these is the Tetragrammaton, YHVH, the four-letter name standing for God, the letters of which represent the eternal and unknowable nature of the Divine. Over the centuries, each of the sefirot came to be associated with a particular name of God that expresses the qualities of that sefirah.

THE SEFIROT ▶
The sefirot are non-material attributes of God.

1 KETER *Crown*
Keter lies at the top of the Tree of Life, in the higher realm of Emanation.

2 CHOKHMAH *Wisdom*
Revelation and inspiration.

3 BINAH *Understanding*
Intellect and reason. In this area also lies **11**, Da'at, the non-sefirah representing knowledge from God.

4 CHESED *Mercy*
Expansive loving-kindness, tolerance.

5 GEVURAH
Judgment or Power
Control, discipline, and discrimination.

6 TIFERET *Beauty*
Equilibrium and grace.

7 NETZACH *Endurance*
Victory, determination, instinctive and impulsive elements.

8 HOD *Glory*
Passive and cognitive energies, prophecy, and communication.

9 YESOD *Foundation*
Generative and reflective energies. Union of feeling, thought, and action.

10 MALKHUT
Kingdom or Presence
Complements Keter, and represents the presence of God in the material world, along with human action.

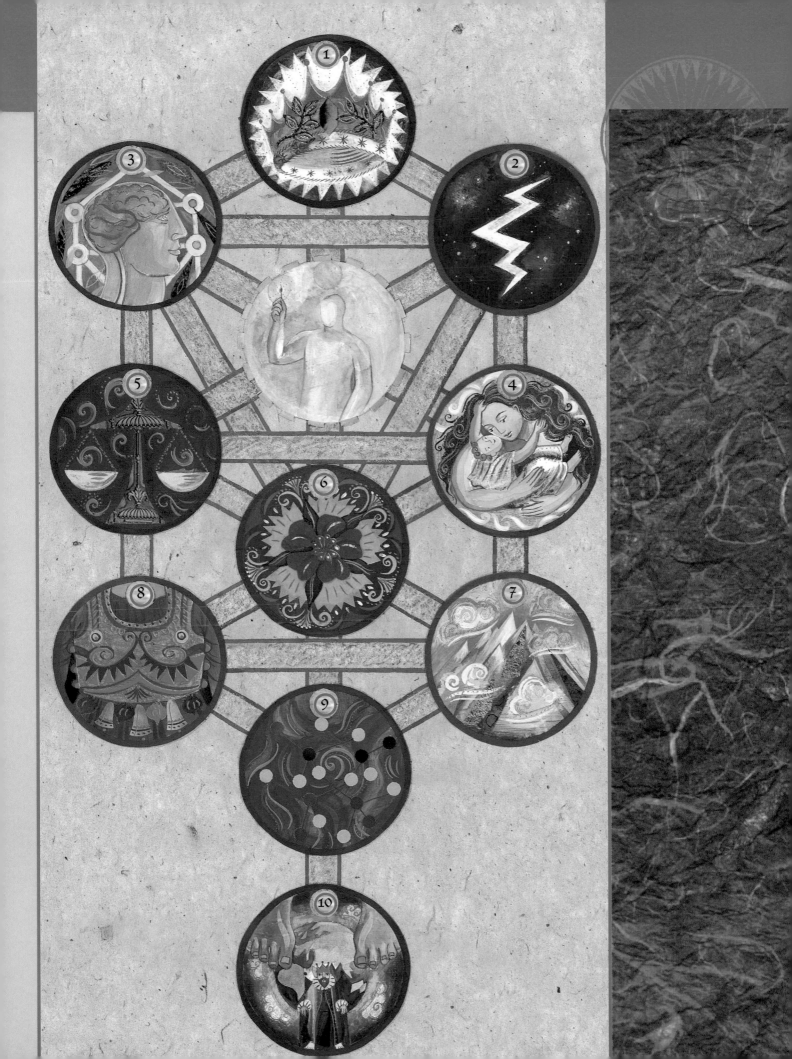

①KETER *Crown*

▲ CROWN OF GOD

Keter represents Divine light and will. Its power is not felt directly in the earthly world, but its essence emanates down through the sefirot.

כתר *The highest of the sefirot is Keter, Crown. Representing the spirit of God and the Divine will, it is the highest rung on the ladder to reaching God. However, God is separate and beyond the sefirot, and the seeker of truth is warned that reaching this sefirah is not the same as knowing God.*

Keter is the root of the Tree of Life and emanating downward from its position at the top. At the same time, it is the goal of spiritual practice. Only the greatest sages are thought capable of achieving this point. Even Moses, with whom God shared the teaching known as the Torah, could not see the face of the Divine, because the light of Keter is too powerful for humanity.

THE SOURCE OF THE SEFIROT

The Kabbalists used the Bible as the source and justification of their metaphysics. The first three sefirot—Keter, Binah, and Chokhmah—and the non-sefirah Da'at are drawn from Exodus:

I have filled him [Bezalel the artist] with the spirit of God, with Wisdom, with Understanding, and with Knowledge.

EXODUS 31:3

▶ FOR THE GLORY OF GOD

Decorative crowns are a traditional adornment for Torah scrolls in synagogues. They remind worshippers that the Torah is at the heart of God's teaching.

KEY WORDS	PERSONIFICATION
Will	Determined leaders (Martin Luther King Jr.)
Inspiration	Visionary leaders (Mahatma Gandhi)
Spirit	Spiritual holy men

CONNECTING THE SEFIROT

Each of the sefirot, except Malkhut, is linked to four or six others, in the form of triads and horizontal, vertical, and diagonal connecting paths. The *Sefer Yetzirah* opens with a statement of how God created the universe:

With thirty-two mystical paths of Wisdom engraved Yah

the Lord of Hosts, the God of Israel, the living God,

King of the Universe, El Shaddai, Merciful and

Gracious, High and Exalted Dwelling in Eternity;

Whose name is Holy; He is lofty and holy; and created

His Universe with three books with text with numbers

and with communication.

SEFER YETZIRAH 1:1

These thirty-two mystical paths refer to the ten sefirot and the twenty-two letters of the Hebrew alphabet, each letter representing one of the paths that link the sefirot. The names of God and the Divine attributes each relate to one of the sefirot.

Each of the sefirot can be understood in terms of their many associations, which demonstrate how pervasive and integral they have become in the Kabbalistic understanding of the universe.

◄ THE COSMIC HEAD

According to Luria, the sefirot are reflections of the face of primordial man. Each sefirah stresses a particular aspect, and on him depends the life of all things. This illustration comes from Kabbala denudata, *1684.*

BEYOND MATERIAL EXISTENCE

These questions will help you find the strengths of Keter and experience a wider, more challenging reality.

✡ *Do you sense that there is a higher purpose in your existence?*

✡ *Do you allow yourself to be inspired?*

✡ *Are you aware that your will is not the Divine will, and that sometimes you may have to choose which to follow?*

ASSOCIATIONS *of* KETER

DIVINE NAME	Ehiyeh asher ehiyeh—I shall be what I shall be, I AM
DIVINE ATTRIBUTE	Equilibrium and the beginning of existence, emanation
COMMANDMENT	I am YHVH, your God
PILLAR	Central, will
COLOR	Blinding white light
PLANET	Neptune or Pluto, depending on the interpretations
TIME	Eternal present
DIRECTION	Good (from *Sefer Yetzirah* 1:5)
ELEMENT	Breath of God, as told by the *Sefer Yetzirah*
ANGEL	Metatron, archangel guarding the throne of God
MUSICAL NOTE	Do
PHYSICAL BODY	Above the head and brain
PSYCHOLOGICAL BODY	Spiritual consciousness, Divine inspiration

ESSENCE *of* KETER

Keter is a living expression of God's will and is elevated far above people.

② CHOKHMAH *Wisdom*

► **TRANSMISSION OF LIGHT**
A flash of lightning is used to represent Chokhmah, because it adds the quality of wisdom to the Divine light of Keter and transmits this power to Binah.

חכמה The second sefirah, Chokhmah (Wisdom), is next after the emanation of Keter (Crown) in the world of Atzilut (Nearness). It is the realm of spirit, but governs the kind of wisdom that comes with revelation and flashes of inspiration. Paired with Binah (Understanding), Chokhmah is on the right pillar of mercy and considered an expression of active masculine energy.

▼ **KING SOLOMON**
King Solomon's eyes are lifted toward God, seeking inspiration.

With Wisdom God established the Earth,

And with Understanding established the Heavens,

And with God's Knowledge, the depths were broken up.

PROVERBS 3:19–20

In the world of Atzilut these sefirot form the source of light in the higher world that illuminates the world of creation. Though the qualities governed by Chokhmah and Binah do not directly affect our physical world, humans aspire to them through study, prayer, and good deeds.

CHOKHMAH PERSONIFIED AS WISDOM

Chokhmah has been identified by some Kabbalists as the primordial Torah (sofia), God's secret wisdom revealed from Nothingness. Although the Torah is considered a feminine word and concept, Chokhmah's position on the Tree indicates the masculine sharing nature of the energy of God's teaching. Human and divine representations are not a part of Jewish art because of the prohibition against graven images; however, later traditions have expressed wisdom as a female form.

▲ **GREEK PARALLELS**
The notion of wisdom was personified in ancient Greek culture by the image of Sophia.

WISDOM OF SOLOMON AND MOSES

King Solomon was seen as a human incarnating the Divine attribute of Chokhmah. The Song of

KEY WORDS	PERSONIFICATION
Wisdom	Philosophers (Confucius, King Solomon)
Revelation	Religious innovators (Buddha)
Light	Inspired philosophers (Plato)
Memory	Community storytellers or shaman

Songs, attributed to him, is the foremost biblical example of love poetry, exemplifying the Divine quality of love that transcends the physical world. Moses is said, in the *Zohar*, to be "hewn from a place [where] no other human was hewn." This has been interpreted to mean that he was created from Chokhmah, unlike other humans, who are formed in the sefirah of Malkhut.

HOLY SPARKS

The *Zohar* indicates that Divine light emanated from God in a blinding flash, one spark that radiated in 370 directions. At first the spark stood still, until a pure aura emerged, whirling, and breathed upon the spark. From the sefirah of Keter the spark moved along the lightning flash to Chokhmah, the place of pure aura, which surrounded and contained the spark. The spark remains hidden and transmits the power of further emanations to Binah.

The work of Kabbalistic unification is to practice right living through contemplation, devotion, and action to reunite these holy sparks.

▶ WISDOM OF THE EAST
Buddha, who achieved enlightenment through his experience of the world and human suffering, may be seen as an Eastern personification of Chokhmah.

GIFT *of* LIGHT

Ask yourself these questions to focus on the possibilities of knowing-beyond-reason:

✿ *Do you ever experience a sudden knowing that appears in a flash?*

✿ *Do you acknowledge and accept the validity of wisdom that comes to you in a non-rational way?*

✿ *Can you ever sense moments when it seems that you are guided and protected by an unseen but appreciable light?*

ESSENCE *of* CHOKHMAH

Chokhmah represents the wisdom that is beyond reason. Spiritual leaders and non-rational philosophers can embody this quality.

ASSOCIATIONS *of* CHOKHMAH

DIVINE NAME	YHVH – Eternal Being of God, Tetragrammaton
DIVINE ATTRIBUTE	Wisdom
COMMANDMENT	You shall have no other gods but me [no idols]
PILLAR	Right, mercy, active expansion
COLOR	Blue or a color including all colors
PLANET	Neptune or Uranus
TIME	Past
DIRECTION	Beginning
ELEMENT	Water from breath
ANGEL	Raziel
MUSICAL NOTE	Re
PHYSICAL BODY	Right ear, right lobe of brain
PSYCHOLOGICAL BODY	Consciousness, spiritual purpose, memory, and revelation

③ BINAH *Understanding*

בינה *Binah (Understanding) lies across from Chokhmah at the top of the passive left pillar of the Tree. Moving from the realm of Atzilut to Beriah, Binah represents the movement of the Divine light into the world of creation. Together these three sefirot comprise the Divine triad in the upper world. Like Keter and Chokhmah, Binah is an essential attribute of creation.*

▸ **REASON AND THOUGHT**
Binah is the sefirah of understanding, which complements and balances the wisdom of Chokhmah. It represents the Divine attribution of reason and thought.

> *With Wisdom a house is built,*
>
> *with Understanding it is established,*
>
> *and with Knowledge its rooms are filled.*
>
> PROVERBS 24:3–4

▸ **PHYSICAL LINK**
In terms of physical correspondences, Binah is associated with the left ear, the left lobe of the brain, and the heart.

Chokhmah has the energy of the father in the upper realm, and is said to impregnate Binah, the upper mother. The energy of Binah allows the conception of a manifestation of God's being. The third sefirah is referred to as the palace and womb in which God's teaching begins to take form. These Divine parents then give birth to their children, the seven lower sefirot.

> *Then this Beginning emanated*
>
> *and made itself a palace for its glory and its praise.*
>
> *There it sowed the seed of its holiness*
>
> *to give birth for the benefit of the Universe.*
>
> *The secret is:*
>
> *"Her stock is a holy seed" (Isaiah 6:13).*
>
> ZOHAR

BALANCING CHOKHMAH AND BINAH

The *Sefer Yetzirah* teaches that the first step in coming close to the sefirot is to understand with wisdom, and to be wise with understanding. Neither the faithful application of rational intellect

KEY WORDS	PERSONIFICATION
Reason	Rational philosophers (Descartes, Maimonides, Aristotle)
Intelligence	Scientists (Albert Einstein, Professor Stephen Hawking)
Language	Innovative teachers or writers (Gertrude Stein, James Joyce)
Palace	Ground-breaking architects (Frank Lloyd Wright)

SPIRITUAL PARALLELS

Seventeenth-century rationalist philosophers taught that only the reasoning powers of humans, not divine revelation, could ascertain truth and regulate human behavior. In the Kabbalistic system, this represents an excess of Binah and a deficiency of Chokhmah.

alone nor the ecstatic devotion of the meditating mystic is sufficient to grasp the intention of the Divine plan. Instead, one must strive intently to explore both verbal and non-verbal, rational and non-rational, consciousness.

TRANSLATING BINAH INTO ACTION

The commandment that accompanies this sefirah is the injunction against taking the name of God in vain. This comes from a clear awareness that careless and uncontrolled thought may lead one to careless speech, which may bring into creation destructive energies that work against the Divine will. This very specific prohibition reminds us that it is both dangerous and misleading to use the Divine name in meditation, prayer, or dealing with people unless there is authentic and complete focus on living in accordance with the Divine will. Such insincere or half-conscious preaching or studying in the name of God results in folly or, worse, destructiveness to self and others.

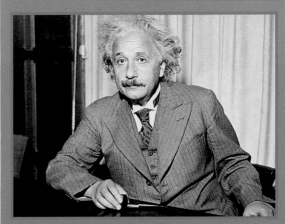

▶ ALBERT EINSTEIN
Einstein formulated the theories of relativity, which revolutionized our understanding of matter, space, and time. He may be seen as an expression of the triumph of rational intellect.

HOW YOU AFFECT YOUR WORLD

Examine the degree of responsibility you take for aspects of your life:

✡ *Consider that your thoughts give birth to reality. Can you maintain awareness of those thoughts to ensure that you are a responsible creator?*

✡ *Does your language reflect a consciousness of purpose and the greater intentions of the universe?*

✡ *What steps can you take to ensure that your thoughts and your intellect are applied with an awareness of higher purpose?*

ASSOCIATIONS of BINAH

DIVINE NAME	Elohim—Creator God (plural) who forms
DIVINE ATTRIBUTE	Understanding
COMMANDMENT	You shall not take the name of YHVH your God in vain
PILLAR	Left, passive, receptive
COLOR	Green and yellow
PLANET	Saturn
TIME	Future
DIRECTION	End
ELEMENT	Fire from water (*Sefer Yetzirah*)
ANGEL	Zaphkiel
MUSICAL NOTE	Mi
PHYSICAL BODY	Left ear, left lobe of brain, heart
PSYCHOLOGICAL BODY	Rational intelligence, verbally constructed thoughts

ESSENCE of BINAH

Binah is the knowledge that falls in the realm of rational intelligence. This quality may be found in scientists, rational philosophers, and writers who use language to explore their understanding of the universe.

④ CHESED *Mercy*

> ▶ SYMBOL OF MERCY
> *The bond between parents and children reflects the special love that humans show toward each other. This love is inspired by the power of Chesed.*

חסד *Chesed is the first of the seven lower sefirot, which connect the upper worlds of Atzilut (Nearness) and Beriah (Creation) to the lower worlds of Yetzirah (Formation) and Assiyah (Action). The qualities of these lower sefirot impinge directly on human life. Divine will begins to take form in Chesed and manifests itself in God's desire to share love.*

DIVINE LOVE AND HUMAN LOVE

The Kabbalists view the love that comes from the Creator as infinite. Flowing down from Keter (Crown), this love permeates the lower worlds and brings with it the possibility that humans can show love and kindness to each other. Chesed refers to acts of loving-kindness and mercy that people can extend to each other in every situation. This expansive love can be seen throughout the Bible, particularly in the Psalms:

> *All the paths of YHVH are mercy and truth*
>
> *for those who keep God's covenant and do*
>
> *God's will.*

> PSALM 25:10

> ▶ SABBATH JOY
> *The Sabbath is a time of joy and rest for the whole family. Traditionally, the father blesses his children on the welcoming in of the Sabbath, exemplifying the loving-kindness associated with Chesed.*

THE LOVING GIFT OF REST

Chesed is associated with the Fourth Commandment, because the Divine gift of rest to the world is an example of God's love. After six days of creating, God blessed what had been done and rested, drawing back from the work of creation and allowing a space for rest and restraint. On the Sabbath, no work is done, the Earth is allowed to rest, and every individual has an opportunity to consider the events of the week gone by in peace and quiet. Meditation, the prayers and readings on Shabbat, and time with family and friends offer a means of achieving balance. Each person is said to be granted an extra soul for the Sabbath, enabling us to enjoy the day on a higher plane than our weekday life.

KEY WORDS	PERSONIFICATION
Loving-kindness	Caregivers (Florence Nightingale), helpful children
Emotion	Mothers with children (Virgin Mary)
Sharing	Philanthropists (Solomon Guggenheim, Andrew Carnegie)

THE LIGHT OF DIVINE LOVE

Divine love is said to manifest itself as symbolic associations of color and light. The vibrational frequencies of the spectrum colors and white (the reflection of all light) and black (the absorption of all light) express the essential quality of each sefirah. On this subject, the *Zohar* invites us to

Come and see: There are four lights.

Three are concealed and one is revealed.

A shining light [Chesed—white]

A glowing light [Gevurah—red]

It shines like the clear brilliance of heaven.

A purple light that absorbs all lights [Tiferet].

A light that does not shine [Shekhinah]

but gazes toward the others and draws them in.

These lights are seen in her as in a crystal facing the

sun. The first three are concealed,

overseeing this one, which is revealed.

ZOHAR

▲ GIVING YOURSELF
Making a conscious and unilateral effort to give your love to others can bring the strength of Chesed closer to your own experience.

The LIGHT THAT *is* LOVE

Look within your heart and answer these questions:

✡ *How does your capacity for love and kindness manifest itself in your daily life?*

✡ *Can you think of times when you have experienced a sense of Divine love and mercy? What effects did it have?*

✡ *Do you choose to give your love and mercy freely to others, or do you wait to receive before you feel safe to share?*

ASSOCIATIONS *of* CHESED

DIVINE NAME	El—Almighty God
DIVINE ATTRIBUTE	Mercy, loving-kindness
COMMANDMENT	Remember the Sabbath day to keep it holy
PILLAR	Right, active, expansive
COLOR	White and silver
PLANET	Jupiter
TIME	Sunday
DIRECTION	South
ELEMENT	None
ANGEL	Zadkiel
MUSICAL NOTE	Fa
PHYSICAL BODY	Right shoulder
PSYCHOLOGICAL BODY	Expression of emotion
PERSONAL CONCERNS	Wisdom

ESSENCE *of* CHESED

Chesed represents the desire to share Divine love with the world. This is represented by those engaged in the caring professions, artists who express their love of life in their work, philanthropists, and those who do good deeds.

⑤ GEVURAH *Judgment*

גבורה *On the left pillar of severity and restriction lies Gevurah, or Judgment, the sefirah that is paired with Chesed (Mercy). It represents a desire to receive judgment and the natural consequences of all actions. The quality of judgment and power must counterbalance mercy and love in order to prevent the Divine light from overwhelming human beings. Similarly, the outreaching mercy of Chesed ensures that the power manifest in Gevurah does not wreak havoc.*

▶ **SCALES OF JUSTICE**
Gevurah holds the attribute of judgment and strength. The proper exercise of judgment requires the ability both to restrain oneself and to judge situations and people where necessary.

THE NATURE OF EVIL

The Kabbalists did not ascribe evil to some external influence in opposition to God. Rather they believed that evil arises from Gevurah (Judgment) and is also an attribute or potential within God itself. In human terms, when the quality of Gevurah is unrestrained, it becomes evil. Thus the archangel associated with this sefirah is Samael (the left hand of God), known as Satan, the Adversary. This understanding of the inherent duality within humanity, as well as within God, was a prescient precursor to the development of psychoanalytic theory in our time.

THE INCLINATION TO GOOD AND EVIL

Within every person, from the age of thirteen, there are said to be two inclinations: *yetzer hatov*, the inclination toward good, and *yetzer hara*, the inclination toward evil. Two angels are said to sit on our shoulders, and each of us must choose at every moment which tendency to follow. Children under thirteen are said to be ruled only by the evil inclination: They do not know the difference between their needs and others' and thus are not responsible for the consequences of their actions.

The balance between Gevurah and Chesed represents a capacity to resist the tendencies to both selfishness and selflessness, extreme poles of the two sefirot.

▶ **THE LAST JUDGMENT**
Christian theology is concerned with the Fall from Grace and the problem with evil, culminating in the apocalyptic Last Judgment. Blake's painting is a powerful expression of the Divine attribute of Gevurah.

SPIRITUAL PARALLELS

Maat, the Egyptian goddess of Justice, Law, and Truth, fulfills a similar role to the principles of Gevurah.

In their Creation stories, the American Iroquois and Huron tribes describe the battle between the twin brothers, Ioskea, the Hero of Creation, and Tawiscara, the Incarnation of Evil. Similarities can be seen with the polarity between Gevurah and Chesed.

ISAAC AND GEVURAH

The *Zohar* associates Gevurah with Isaac, the son of Abraham. Abraham is linked with Chesed for his generosity, and also because his love of God was so great that he was prepared to sacrifice his son at God's command. Perhaps also, the Kabbalists recognized the potential power of Isaac's anger at what had almost been done to him.

Out of the scorching noon of Isaac,

out of the dregs of wine, a fungus emerged, a cluster,

male and female together, red as a rose,

expanding in many directions and paths.

ZOHAR 1:148B

▶ BRINGING WISDOM INTO JUDGMENT
Abraham was called by God to sacrifice his beloved son, Isaac. However, God restrained Abraham from killing the boy by providing a ram in the thicket, showing a shift from one Divine attribute to another.

KEY WORDS	PERSONIFICATION
Power	Professional fighters or boxers, corporate leaders (Bill Gates)
Judgment	Royal or civil judges (Queen Elizabeth I, Abraham Lincoln)
Fire	Military scientists (Robert Oppenheimer)
Evil	Brutal dictators (Stalin)

JUDGMENT *in* BALANCE

Be willing to examine your thoughts and deeds as you ask yourself these questions:

✡ *Are you quick to judge others and criticize, or do you exercise restraint over your judgments?*

✡ *Do you see yourself as one who primarily receives or gives in relationships? Is there a way that you can begin to balance the two tendencies?*

✡ *Do you know when you are making a deliberate choice for good or evil? Do you try to justify the choices that are selfish or wrong?*

ESSENCE *of* GEVURAH

Gevurah is the strength that comes from the ability to judge and to use the power of judgment to make an impact on the world. These qualities may be expressed by major political leaders and those people, however ordinary, who use their inner strength in the world.

ASSOCIATIONS *of* GEVURAH

DIVINE NAME	Yah—Eternal God Who is to be praised
DIVINE ATTRIBUTE	Judgment, power
COMMANDMENT	Honor your father and your mother
PILLAR	Left, severity, restriction
COLOR	Red and gold
PLANET	Mars
TIME	Monday
DIRECTION	North
ELEMENT	Isaac
ANGEL	Samael
MUSICAL NOTE	Sol
PHYSICAL BODY	Left shoulder
PSYCHOLOGICAL BODY	Control and discrimination
PERSONAL CONCERNS	Wealth, love

⑥ TIFERET *Beauty*

▶ METAPHYSICAL
CENTER
*Tiferet is at the center of
the self and the center of
the Tree of Life. It holds
the whole structure
together.*

תפארת *The sefirah that forms a triad with
mercy and judgment is Tiferet, meaning
Beauty. It creates harmony between those
two poles and also forms the link between
the two worlds of Yetzirah (Formation)
and Assiyah (Action). Tiferet represents
the beauty of Divine glory and light as it
descends to humanity. It also links the
psychological self of Yetzirah (Formation)
to the spiritual self in Beriah (Creation).*

Tiferet is the center of the Tree of Life,
channeling the Divine Spirit downward, and the
spiritual aspirations of humanity upward.

JACOB AND TIFERET

Jacob is seen by the Kabbalists as the representation of Tiferet. Despite his flawed human actions,
Jacob also wrestled with the angel of God and was
renamed Yisrael, meaning the one who struggles
with God, Israel. He was said to balance the two
polar qualities of judgment and mercy.

Inside the hidden nexus [sefirot],

From within the sealed secret [the top triad],

a zohar flashed [first rays of Tiferet],

shining as a mirror, embracing two colors

blended together [yellow and purple] …

In this zohar dwells the one who dwells [Ayn Sof].

It provides a name for the one who is concealed

and totally unknown.

It is called the Voice of Jacob [Tiferet].

ZOHAR 1:147A

▶ COLORS OF BEAUTY
*The exquisite beauty
and complex structure of
peacock feathers is a
manifestation of Tiferet
in our world.*

Tiferet links directly to all the other sefirot except
Malkhut (Kingdom). In the ascent to spiritual
understanding, human beings must rise above
their personal emotional concerns and become one
with the self that is an expression of the Divine. In
this sense, Tiferet provides a mirror that reflects
the Divine light and also enables the righteous to

KEY WORDS	PERSONIFICATION
Beauty	Perceptive and emotional artists (Beethoven, Chagall, Shakespeare)
Center or equilibrium	Tightrope walkers, ballet dancers (Mikhail Baryshnikov)
Heart	Artists whose work reflects personal experiences (Barbra Streisand, Steven Spielberg)

see their own beauty reflected. Likewise, it is the balancing point between the active and passive qualities of the Divine and the human being, and is thus the means of keeping the sefirot in balance.

WHAT BELONGS TO HUMANITY?

The Kabbalists emphasized the importance of maintaining a focused intention based on contemplation, prayer, and good deeds in order to prevent a slide into misguided arrogance or evil. At all times one must remember that God is the Source of all, and union with God (Yichud) is the goal of all spiritual enterprise. King David made it clear that everything came from the Divine:

Yours, oh YHVH, is the greatness (Gevurah)

and the glory (Tiferet) and the victory (Netzach)

and the majesty (Hod). For everything that is Heaven

and Earth is yours.

I CHRONICLES 29:11

▲ AT THE HEART OF LIFE
Balancing judgment and loving-kindness, the best teachers bring wisdom and understanding to the task of enabling children to learn to express their creativity and beauty.

BEAUTY *at* YOUR CENTER

Discern beyond the physical when you answer these questions:

✿ *Does beauty play a central part in your life?*

✿ *If not, what can you do to allow yourself to open to the beauty of nature, humanity, and the universe?*

✿ *Are you able to recognize the beauty within yourself and allow it to shine outward?*

ASSOCIATIONS *of* TIFERET

DIVINE NAME	YHVH Elohim, Adonai Elohim or Eternal God of Creation
DIVINE ATTRIBUTE	Beauty
COMMANDMENT	You shall not murder
PILLAR	Central
COLOR	Yellow and purple
PLANET	Sun
TIME	Tuesday
DIRECTION	East
ELEMENT	Jacob
ANGEL	Michael
MUSICAL NOTE	Half-tone interval
PHYSICAL BODY	Below heart, over solar plexus
PSYCHOLOGICAL BODY	Self
PERSONAL CONCERNS	Children and grace

ESSENCE *of* TIFERET

Tiferet is the intermediary between Chesed and Gevurah. People manifesting this quality are centered in their understanding of life. These include artists, musicians, film-makers, and those whose goal is to express beauty and truth in their work and offer it to humanity.

⑦ NETZACH *Eternity*

► DIVINE VICTORY
Netzach expresses the energy of determination that inspires people to change the world, either for better or worse.

נצח *The seventh sefirah, on the right pillar of expansiveness, is Netzach, or Eternity; the lasting endurance or victory of God. It represents the compassionate rule of God, balanced by Hod (Glory or Reverberation) on the left pillar. Netzach and Hod symbolize the right and left legs, superimposed on the body of Adam Kadmon, the primordial human being.*

MOSES AND NETZACH

Moses was able to channel the Divine teaching to the people. Through his faith and devotion, he led his people into the unknown future, to a new relationship with God. For these qualities, Moses is seen to represent eternity, and Jewish people marry today "according to the law of Moses," thus entering into a lasting relationship. For this reason, Netzach is associated with the Seventh Commandment, "You shall not commit adultery," stressing that the responsibility for maintaining relationships depends on commitment to loyalty and eternity.

expression of the energy of Netzach, maintaining a self-perpetuating system. The interference of humanity in these systems, resulting in imbalance, destruction, and extinction, demonstrates the danger of unconscious tinkering with nature based on an arrogant belief that knowledge or ability justifies all actions.

► CROSSING THE JORDAN
After 40 years of wandering, the Israelites are led across the Jordan into the promised land. The enduring quality of Netzach can be seen in their entrance into their new homeland.

THE NATURAL WORLD

In the realm of nature, Netzach is the active principle underlying the systems within organisms and the psychobiological processes of life. The interdependent and carefully balanced ecological systems are an

KEY WORDS	PERSONIFICATION
Eternity	Monarchs remembered throughout history (Cleopatra, Alexander the Great, Louis XIV)
Prophesy	Great prophets (Moses, Muhammad)
Victory	Warriors and military leaders (George Washington, Winston Churchill, samurai warriors)

47

The Sefirot

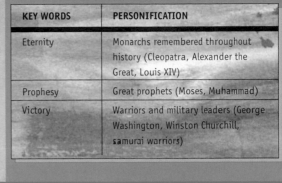

EXPERIENCING NETZACH

On an emotional level, Netzach represents the desires of the ego and must be carefully monitored by the responses of Hod (Reverberation) to prevent the body from going into self-seeking overdrive. The positive qualities of Netzach may be experienced as conscious actions, stepping forward in life to express the will of the individual. Without the energy of this sefirah, there would be no motivation to succeed in life or to make a personal contribution.

THE WORD

The word *Netzach* does not appear in the Torah, but farther on in the Book of Samuel and some of the later writings. In many of its uses, the word refers to negative behavior and destruction.

> *God will destroy death forever [Netzach]*
>
> *And the Lord God will wipe away tears*
>
> *from all faces.*

ISAIAH 25:8

BEYOND *the* PRESENT MOMENT

Open up to the greater metaphysical reality as you ask yourself these questions:

✡ *What does "forever" mean to you?*

✡ *Are you driven by a desire to make a permanent mark on life, to leave a sign of your having been here?*

✡ *Do you allow the idea of eternity to influence your thoughts and feelings, or do you live only in the present?*

ESSENCE *of* NETZACH

Netzach represents the outgoing quality of the ego, expressed by those who desire to change the world forever by their presence.

ASSOCIATIONS *of* NETZACH

DIVINE NAME	YHVH Tzva'ot—God of Hosts
DIVINE ATTRIBUTE	Eternity, victory
COMMANDMENT	You shall not commit adultery
PILLAR	Right, mercy, expansion
COLOR	Light pink
PLANET	Venus
TIME	Wednesday
DIRECTION	None
ELEMENT	Moses
ANGEL	Haniel
MUSICAL NOTE	La
PHYSICAL BODY	Right hip/thigh
PSYCHOLOGICAL BODY	Support and determination
PERSONAL CONCERNS	Life and health

⑧HOD *Glory*

▶ **THE ADORNMENTS OF AARON**
Hod is the eighth sefirah and represents the Divine qualities of glory and splendor. It is represented by the jeweled breast-plate of the high priest Aaron.

הוד Balanced against Netzach is Hod, the Glory, Reverberation, Honor, and Splendor of the Divine. On the passive left pillar, Hod represents, in the world of Assiyah (Action), the thinking processes that channel Divine inspiration into prophecy and the monitoring systems that keep in check the tendency to create and act for the sake of self.

When God instructed Moses to choose Joshua as the next leader of the people, Moses was told, "And give some of your honor (Hod) onto him, so that all the congregation … may be obedient." The splendor of Hod has a purpose: to ensure that the Divine will is understood and obeyed.

AARON AS THE EMBODIMENT OF HOD

As the high priest of the Temple, Aaron was able to express Divine will in a way that the people could understand and embodied the restrained qualities of Hod. His glory and splendor were not for his own sake, but to serve the will of his Creator.

Like Aaron, we must exercise restraint and monitor the motives behind the honor we seek and the splendor with which we present ourselves. On the other hand, this sefirah is the channel for inspiration, and we can receive its benefit if we pay close attention to our motivation and daily practice. Failure to do so risks the appearance of dangerous false prophets.

◀ **THE THINKER**
Rodin's extraordinary sculpture of The Thinker *expresses the left pillar of the Tree of Life and the combined attributes Binah, Gevurah, and Tiferet.*

YOU SHALL NOT STEAL

The Eighth Commandment is linked with Hod because the knowledge gained through thought, study, and from others must not be misused. We must take responsibility for how we gain and use our knowledge. Hod, as the channel of knowledge of what is right, offers a counterpoint to Netzach (Eternity), where personal desires may overwhelm the individual.

The splendor of Hod channels light to Shekhinah, the feminine presence of God dwelling in the sefirah of Malkhut (Kingdom). The immanent presence of Shekhinah touches the prophets of the world and makes truth clearer.

All the prophets of the world were nurtured from a

single aspect

through two well-known levels [Hod and Netzach].

Those levels appeared in the mirror that does not

shine [Shekhinah],

as it is written:

"I make Myself known to him in a vision [mar'ah]."

What is this mar'ah?

It has been explained: a mirror in which all colors

appear [Shekhinah].

This is the mirror that does not shine.

ZOHAR 1:183A

KEY WORDS	PERSONIFICATION
Splendor	Religious leaders (the Pope, Aaron the high priest)
Communication	Great communicators (Martin Luther King Jr.)
Responsibility	Idealists (Ralph Nader, Dalai Lama)

▲ PROTECTIVE SYMBOLS

Aaron's resplendent robes are said to have been adorned with bells and pomegranates to prevent him being struck dead by the glory of God. Bells still play a role in the synagogue and are used to decorate the Torah scrolls.

FOUNDED *on* INTEGRITY

These questions will help you to perceive what underlies your actions:

✡ *For what purpose do you acquire and use knowledge?*

✡ *Do you credit the sources of your knowledge and refrain from stealing other people's ideas?*

✡ *Are you overly concerned with looking good to make an impression or manipulate others?*

ESSENCE *of* HOD

Hod is not splendor for personal satisfaction or glory for its own sake, but an expression of higher will. People demonstrating this attribute have a vision of a better world.

ASSOCIATIONS *of* HOD

DIVINE NAME	Elohim Tzva'ot—Creator God of Hosts
DIVINE ATTRIBUTE	Glory, majesty, splendor, reverberation
COMMANDMENT	You shall not steal
PILLAR	Left, severity, restriction
COLOR	Dark pink
PLANET	Mercury
TIME	Thursday
DIRECTION	Down
ELEMENT	Aaron
ANGEL	Raphael (healing)
MUSICAL NOTE	Ti
PHYSICAL BODY	Left hip/thigh
PSYCHOLOGICAL BODY	Support
PERSONAL CONCERNS	Dominance, advancement

⑨ YESOD *Foundation*

▸ **FOUNDATION OF LIFE**

Yesod is the basis on which life is built, represented here by one of the molecular structures that determine our existence.

▾ **REPRODUCTIVE POWERS**

The position of Yesod on the Tree of Life is associated with the genitals. Our reproductive powers remind us of the intricate complexities and foundation of the life of the whole society.

יסוד *The ninth sefirah, Yesod, is placed on the central pillar and represents the foundation of everything in the world of Assiyah (Action). Illustrated as the genitals of* Adam Kadmon, *or primordial man, Yesod provides the energy of creation and is the intermediary between Hod (Glory) and Netzach (Eternity).*

PSYCHOANALYTIC AND KABBALISTIC STRUCTURES

On a psychological level, Yesod (Foundation) expresses the energy of the unconscious mind, which directs action according to needs that may not be part of conscious awareness. In psychoanalytic terms, this is called the id. Although it is necessary for the individual life force to find expression, the power of this energy must be balanced by the conscious self (ego) and the conscience (superego). In Kabbalistic terms, Yesod is the channel for the Divine creativity and life force to come down into the world of Assiyah, where it can find expression in all aspects of human life. Sexual potency guarantees the union of male and female energies for creativity, which is an assertion of both. Yesod is the procreative power of God, where Divine light is waiting to burst forth.

The light created by the Blessed Holy One

in the act of Creation flared from one end

of the world to the other

and was hidden away.

Why was it hidden away?

So the wicked of the world would not enjoy it

and the world would not enjoy it because of them.

It is stored away for the righteous,

for the Righteous One [Yesod].

As it is written:

"Light is sown for the righteous one,

joy for the upright in heart" [Psalm 97:11].

Then the worlds will be fragrant, and all will be one.

But until the day when the world that is coming

arrives, it is stored and hidden away …

ZOHAR 2:148B

JOSEPH AND YESOD

In the Genesis story, Joseph is accosted by Potiphar's wife, who attempts to seduce him. The rabbis saw his refusal of her advances as evidence that Joseph could control his sexual urges and resist temptation. He is therefore referred to as the Righteous One [tzaddik] and came to be seen as the figure best expressing the qualities of self-control and sexual restraint. Furthermore, in his job as steward of Egypt, Joseph was responsible for the food supply for the country during the famine.

KEY WORDS	PERSONIFICATION
Foundation	Universal visionaries (Leonardo da Vinci, Karl Marx, Charles Darwin)
Sexuality	Sexual theorists and counselors (Freud, Dr. Ruth Westheimer)
Speaking the truth	Fearless rebels (Sir Thomas More, social reformer Susan B. Anthony)

◄ HIGH ABOVE
Linked to Yesod, the moon is the governor of emotion and sexuality. Created as the lesser light to rule over the world, it is also associated with the unconscious mind.

DIRECTING YOUR LIFE FORCE

Delve beyond the surface with these questions to discover what basic motives drive you:

✧ *What lies at the foundation of your four worlds?*

✧ *Do you attend to the work necessary to build foundations before results, or are you mainly concerned with results?*

✧ *Do you balance your sexual needs against the needs of others? Do you exercise restraint or give in to the passions of the moment?*

ASSOCIATIONS *of* YESOD

DIVINE NAME	El Chai Shaddai—Almighty Living God
DIVINE ATTRIBUTE	Foundation
COMMANDMENT	You shall not bear false witness against your neighbor
PILLAR	Central
COLOR	Orange or black
PLANET	Moon
TIME	Friday
DIRECTION	West
ELEMENT	Joseph
ANGEL	Gavriel – Strength of God, spiritual knowledge
MUSICAL NOTE	Half-tone interval
PHYSICAL BODY	Genitals
PSYCHOLOGICAL BODY	Union of feeling, thought, and action
PERSONAL CONCERNS	Peace

ESSENCE *of* YESOD

Yesod expresses the foundation on which all the creativity of the real world is based. People manifesting this quality combine the attributes of both the left and right pillars of the Tree of Life and bring them into form. They may be scientists, philosophers, designers, and those who create and explain the diversity of life.

⑩ MALKHUT *Kingdom*

▶ OUR WORLD

Malkhut is the realm in which humanity exists. While every human soul is created in the seventh heaven of Beriah, it is the union of man and woman that brings that soul's existence into Malkhut as a human being.

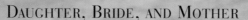

מלכות *The tenth sefirah is Malkhut, the Kingdom, which is also known as Shekhinah, the feminine presence of God. The early rabbis did not view the Shekhinah as a woman, but rather as the feminine energy of Nearness (Atzilut), the immanence of God. Once part of the Divine will, after the dispersion of the holy sparks, the Shekhinah descended to humanity to be a vessel for Divine light.*

DAUGHTER, BRIDE, AND MOTHER

The Kabbalists conceived of the Shekhinah as one of the ten children of the union between Chokhmah (Wisdom) and Binah (Understanding). It is also seen as the partner of Tiferet (Beauty), and the energy required for their union, which is seen as one of dynamic tension, is channeled by Yesod (Foundation). Together they bear the human soul, in the world of Assiyah (Action).

Some of the names applied to Shekhinah include Lower Mother, Princess, Bride, Queen, Rachel, Earth, Rose, Throne of Glory, Garden of Eden, Holy Apple Orchard, and Moon. Although she has no Divine attribute of her own, the Shekhinah sustains the lower worlds and is the feminine indwelling presence of God that hovers in Malkhut. It is perceived as Malkhut, but not identical to it.

Shekhinah is embodied in the oral Torah, the traditional interpretations and stories passed down through the generations, whereas her partner Tiferet is embodied in the written Torah. For Kabbalists, the attainment of this union became one of the goals of Yichud, the work of unification.

TIME, DIRECTION, AND THE PLANETS

The Earth, the center of our existence, is the planet linked with Malkhut, and represents the grounded, mortal nature of human beings. Through attention to our own planet, we learn what right action is, and find our connections with the rest of the universe. Human life on Earth is the only thing that we can really come close to; therefore, the center is the direction linked to Malkhut. The work of the student of Kabbalah is to raise the level of everyday life to an harmonious integration of the energies of all the sefirot.

Saturday is associated with this sefirah. In the mundane world of struggle, the Sabbath points up most clearly the importance of maintaining equilibrium between action and refraining from action. On this day, one refrains from all attempts to make a human mark on the world.

KING DAVID AND MALKHUT

David was a young military hero, a poet, a lover, a great king and strategist, and a leader almost larger than life. His ability to lead was overshadowed by the weaknesses of his character, which

SPIRITUAL PARALLELS

The Hindu notion of Krishna as the earthly manifestation of the Divine presence is almost identical to the Shekhinah of Malkhut.

led him to deception and murder. Thus he was considered unfit to build the Temple in Jerusalem. He struggled in his life and in his poetry, the Psalms, to reconcile the two tendencies, toward good and toward evil. For this reason he is seen as a reflection of the daily struggle in which we all engage.

KEY WORDS	PERSONIFICATION
Fruit of the Tree of Life	Men and women with life-giving talents, such as doctors and cooks; the first humans, Adam and Eve
Earth	Individuals whose ethics and inner strengths have helped change history (Oskar Schindler, John F. Kennedy, Thomas Edison, archeologists)
Breath	Politicians and singers who express their ideas through their vocal talents (Martin Luther King Jr., Elton John, Madonna)

◄ THE WEALTH OF LIFE

Life on Earth often seems the center of our universe, as daily concerns and the political and ecological state of the world can make all the difference to the future of humanity.

ASSOCIATIONS *of* MALKHUT

DIVINE NAME	Adonai—My Lord
DIVINE ATTRIBUTE	Kingdom
COMMANDMENT	You shall not covet anything that belongs to your neighbor
PILLAR	Central
COLOR	Blue
PLANET	Earth
TIME	Saturday
DIRECTION	Center
ELEMENT	Air (breath)
ANGEL	Sandalphon
MUSICAL NOTE	Do
PHYSICAL BODY	Between the feet
PSYCHOLOGICAL BODY	None
PERSONAL CONCERNS	Grace, attractiveness

YOUR WORK *in* THIS WORLD

Discover whether your work is attuned to the Divine will by answering these questions:

✡ *Do you consider the work of your hands, mind, and heart of equal importance?*

✡ *What can you do to ensure that you consider the higher purpose that resides in all the work that you are called upon to do?*

✡ *Have you ever tried to discover if you are called to a particular kind of work, and for what purpose?*

ESSENCE *of* MALKHUT

Malkhut is the level of ordinary daily living that we all inhabit. Its attributes are expressed by those who use their talents to do something real in life. They may be great or evil people, but often ordinary folk whose actions can make a difference to the world.

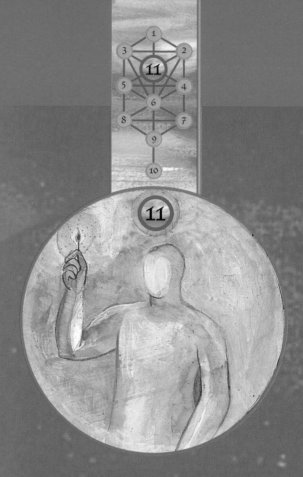

⑪ DA'AT *Knowledge*

54

The Tree of Life

> ▶ **THE NON-SEFIRAH**
> *The notion of Da'at is based on the* Sefer Yetzirah, *which tells us to "understand with wisdom and be wise with understanding." This non-sefirah is placed on the central pillar between Keter and Tiferet, Binah, and Chokhmah.*

> ▼ **SPARK OF DA'AT**
> *A single flame or spark represents the ethereal space of Da'at. The knowledge of Da'at is not a human quality, but Divine energy located in the center of the Tree.*

דעת *One of the most mysterious aspects of the sefirotic system is Da'at, or Knowledge, the invisible non-sefirah. It lies on the central pillar, between Keter (Crown) and Tiferet (Beauty). It is seen to unify the opposing energies of Chokhmah (Wisdom) and Binah (Understanding) into a knowledge of the Divine will that is transmitted through Tiferet and Yesod (Foundation), to their offspring in the human realm of Malkhut (Kingdom).*

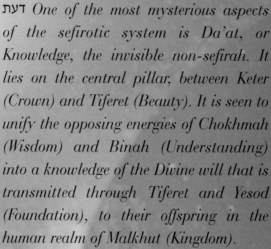

Da'at is the empty space wherein creation begins. God's will and grace emanate down from the roots of Keter in Atzilut (Nearness), and are called into being in the world of Beriah (Creation). The *Sefer Yetzirah* makes it clear that Da'at is not one of the sefirot:

> *Ten Sefirot of Nothingness*
>
> *ten and not nine,*
>
> *ten and not eleven.*
>
> SEFER YETZIRAH 1:4

DA'AT IN THE GARDEN OF EDEN

Da'at represents the knowledge that comes directly from the Divine. It is the combination of knowledge that comes from wisdom and understanding, but it is not a human quality. Da'at first appears in the Bible in Chapter Two of Genesis, when God placed the Tree of Knowledge [Da'at] of Good and Evil in the center of the garden, along with the Tree of Life and every other tree good to see and eat. All the other trees were offered to Adam as food, but the Tree of Knowledge of Good and Evil was to be avoided, as eating from it would result in death. The knowledge of God was too overwhelming for humans at this infant stage of their development. Knowledge of Good and Evil is now a part of human consciousness, as a result of the Fall that came from eating the fruit. Knowledge of the Divine is the aim of Kabbalah, and this is expressed as Yichud, or unification with God. However, Kabbalah recognizes that humans can only attempt to experience Divine union.

The word *da'at* next appears in Exodus, when God imbued the great artist Bezalel with the Divine attributes of Chokhmah (Wisdom), Binah (Understanding), and Da'at. Bezalel was to be charged with the task of supervising and creating the great Tabernacle to hold the Ark of the Divine teaching, and could only do so if he could understand what God wanted.

KEY WORDS	PERSONIFICATION
Knowledge	Prophets, mystics, Bezalel, fortune-tellers, shamans, and diviners
Invisible	None

▲ THE TORAH AS TREE OF LIFE
The Torah is called a "tree of life to all who grasp it, and those who hold fast to it are happy. Its ways are ways of pleasantness and all its paths are peace."

The MYSTERY of KNOWLEDGE

These questions can help you learn the different ways that knowledge can manifest itself:

✡ *Can you direct your heart to the place of Nothingness in order to be open to Divine knowledge?*

✡ *Do you allow your throat to expand through song, chanting, humming, to enable the voice of the Shekhinah to be heard?*

✡ *If you dedicate your life to spiritual study and practice, can you imagine one day being ready to meditate on the Nothingness of Ayn Sof?*

ASSOCIATIONS of DA'AT

DIVINE NAME	None
DIVINE ATTRIBUTE	Knowledge, voice of Shekhinah
COMMANDMENT	None
PILLAR	Central
COLOR	None
PLANET	None
TIME	None
DIRECTION	None
ELEMENT	None
ANGEL	None
MUSICAL NOTE	Half-tone interval
PHYSICAL BODY	Throat
PSYCHOLOGICAL BODY	None
PERSONAL CONCERNS	None

ESSENCE of DA'AT

Da'at is the non-sefirah that mediates between Binah and Chokhmah. It is represented by great thinkers who combine both reflective, intuitive wisdom and rational intellect to channel Divine light into the world and raise the physical work of humanity to a higher spiritual level.

CHAPTER THREE

THE PATHS

The Tree of Life is a dynamic and interconnected system. Within each of the four worlds, the Tree consists of the ten sefirot linked by paths. The beginning of the Sefer Yetzirah explains that God created the universe with thirty-two paths of wisdom. These paths comprise the ten sefirot and the twenty-two letters of the Hebrew alphabet that connect them. These are the paths that we walk every day. This chapter examines their meaning.

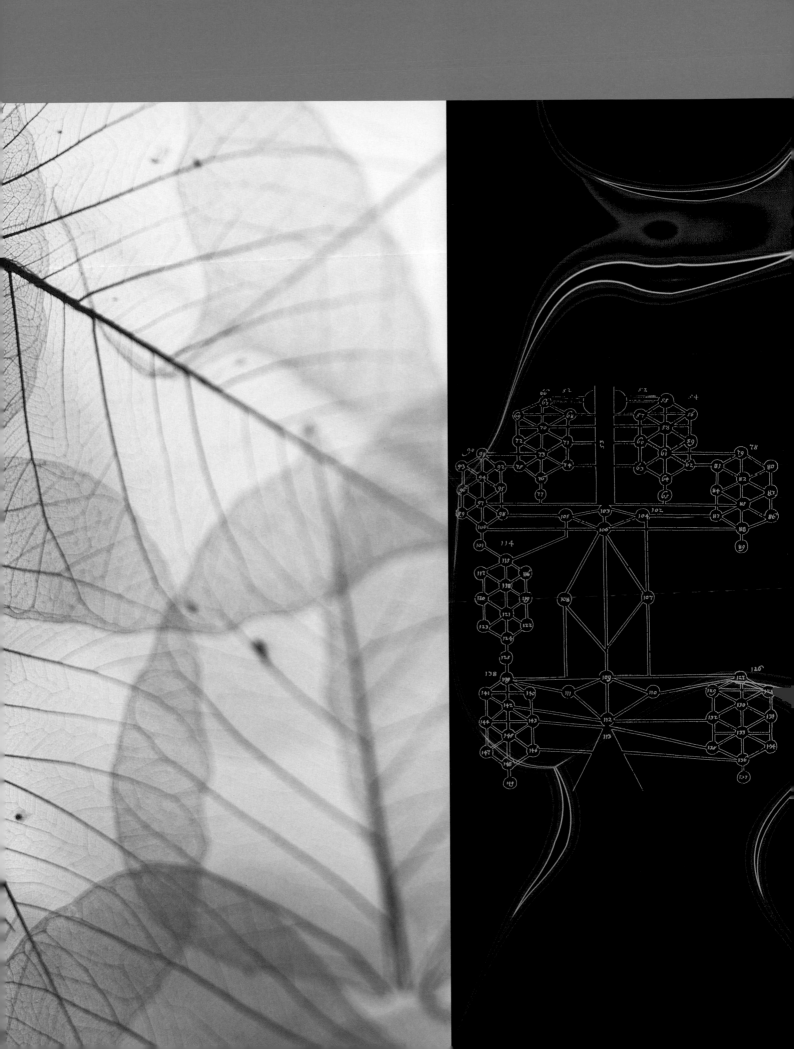

THE THREE MOTHERS

Linking and holding the two-way flow of energy between the sefirot are the paths. Each path is represented by one of the sefirot or by a Hebrew letter. The three mother letters are alef, *the first letter of the Hebrew alphabet,* mem, *the thirteenth letter, and* shin, *the penultimate, twenty-first letter. The letters are described in the* Sefer Yetzirah *as having been engraved and carved by the breath of God.*

▶ IMAGE OF DNA
The structure of DNA shows similarities to the Tree of Life: DNA's horizontal bars carry the essential genetic code, while the Tree of Life's horizontal paths connect the left and right pillars.

THESIS—ANTITHESIS—SYNTHESIS

The three mother letters form the foundation structure of the Tree of Life and sefirot. There are two different ways of viewing the structure. In one approach, *mem* represents the right column, or pillar—Chokhmah (Wisdom), Chesed (Mercy), and Netzach (Eternity). It can be viewed elementally as water and in philosophical terms as thesis, the first statement of Divine teaching. *Shin* represents the left pillar—Binah (Understanding), Gevurah (Judgment), and Hod (Glory). It is the element of fire, and its philosophical position is that of antithesis, the statement of teaching that appears to contradict the first one. *Alef* oversees the central pillar—Keter (Crown), Tiferet (Beauty), Yesod (Foundation), and lastly Malkhut (Kingdom)—and can be seen as synthesis, the third teaching that resolves the apparent contradiction or paradox between the first two. *Alef* is the element of air, and is often referred to as the "soundless sound before the first sound" was uttered, the breath of God.

SPANNING THE PILLARS

According to the great sixteenth-century Kabbalist Isaac Luria, the three mothers are the horizontal lines that span the pillars and link opposing sefirot: *Shin* links Chokhmah and Binah; *alef* connects Chesed and Gevurah; *mem* joins Netzach and Hod. In this system, thesis is the right-hand sefirah, antithesis is the left-hand sefirah, and synthesis is the mother letter connecting the two. The Lurianic system is the one used throughout this book.

BALANCE BETWEEN MERIT AND LIABILITY

The two "pans" mentioned in the opening quotation (left) are as on a balance scale, holding or weighing the merits and sins of the universe. The "tongue of decree" is the indicator on a balance that shows equilibrium or disequilibrium. However, the tongue can also refer to the human tongue, which can balance the actions of the two sides of one's nature.

HUM, HISS, AND BREATH OF AIR

The three descriptions of the sounds made by the letters—hum, hiss, and breath of air—are in fact a guide to using them as a meditative route to spiritual balance. Apart from the alliterative link between the Hebrew words and the three letters, they are also onomatopoeic: the sound *m* is hummed, *sh* is hissed, and *ah* is breathed. By humming the *mem* (*m*) sound, one can attain calmness, associated with water and the con-

The three mother letters are Alef Mem Shin.
Their foundation is a pan of merit, a pan of liability:
And the tongue of decree deciding between them.
Mem hums, *Shin* hisses, *and* Alef *is the breath of air deciding between them.*

SEFER YETZIRAH 2:1

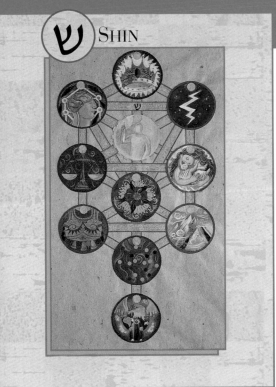

sciousness of Chokhmah, which is wisdom. These show parallels with the chanting of the Sanskrit mantra *om*.

SHIN ש

Shin, pronounced *sh*, has the numerical value of 300 (see pages 94–97). It is linked to *ruach Elohim*, which means the *spirit* or *breath of God*, which also has the numerical total of 300. *Shin* connects to fire (in Hebrew, *aish*) and Binah. By repeating that sound, the Kabbalist can approach the consciousness of Binah—a clearer understanding of teaching and truth—which can then be applied through language to life. Fire, as in other spiritual traditions, is an element of transformation, allowing the new to be created from the dissociation of the old. In alchemy, fire refines, and here one's understanding of the Divine purpose can be refined through this technique.

There are several significant interpretations made from the two mother letters *shin* and *mem*. Together they spell *shem* which means *name* and is used instead of the name of God. Using names enables a person to know and understand the world and thus connects to Chokhmah and Binah.

The second, more esoteric connection is with the word *chashmal*, meaning *amber*. Aryeh Kaplan notes that the Kabbalists view this as the "interface between the physical and the spiritual,

seen by Ezekiel the prophet in the middle of a vision of fire." Interestingly, amber is the substance that preserves prehistoric fossil material, and in the Steven Spielberg movie *Jurassic Park* it preserved the dinosaur DNA, thus forming the link between the physical structure of the dinosaurs of the past, and the spiritual and moral issue of re-creating them in the present.

Alef, the soundless letter that begins the Hebrew alphabet, is expressed as breath; air is most often breathed unconsciously, an expression of Chokhmah. However, by controlling one's breath, a person can move toward Binah.

A SENSE *of* BALANCE

These questions will help you recognize the link between your physical and spiritual reality:

✿ *How do you feel and what do you think when you hum, hiss, and breathe with your voice?*

✿ *How do you imagine that a balance scale of your merits and demerits would look at this moment?*

✿ *Consider how your breathing is an expression of your spiritual as well as your physical well-being. What can you do to control your breathing and thus influence your health?*

CHANNELS *of* ENERGY *and* BALANCE

The sefirot represent the perfection of God's essence. That Divine essence is transmitted along the paths from Keter down to Malkhut. Additionally, humanity passes along the paths as it aspires to God. Each path plays a role in the transmission of energy and in the balance between the sefirot. As one sefirah turns toward another, there is a separate channel of influence.

Several Hebrew words for path are used in the Bible. The term in the *Sefer Yetzirah* is *nativ*, which refers to a private path. The numerical value of this word is 462 (see pages 94–97), which is twice the number of the 231 gates described in Chapter 2:4 of that book. This implies that traveling the paths through the 231 gates is the lifetime task of anyone wishing to ascend through the gates to union with the Divine light.

ALEF א

Alef, the first letter of the Hebrew alphabet, is overlaid with mystical interpretation. Although it corresponds to the vowel *a* in the English alphabet, the letter is silent in Hebrew, and only takes on pronunciation when a consonant or another vowel is attached to it. *Alef* is thought to have existed before sound, the breath of God, who began the creation of the universe by transforming the Atzilutic will into the Beriatic act of creation by breathing the *alef*.

The *Sefer Yetzirah* says that God "made the letter *alef* king over breath [the Hebrew, *ruach*, also means *spirit*] and bound a crown to it." Thus the power of Keter, at the top of the Tree of Life, is linked to human kingship in Malkhut, where Divine will can be expressed or manifested. It also

traverses the chest on the image of the human body, overseeing the act of breathing.

To begin to understand the energy of *alef*:
✿ focus your mind on your essential nature, that which existed before you were even born;
✿ open your mouth and relax your throat, allowing air to escape with a voiced sound *aaah*;
✿ as you breathe this *aaah*, be aware of where you feel it in your body and mind;
✿ allow the power of the sound to connect and balance your own energies of judgment (Gevurah) and mercy (Chesed).

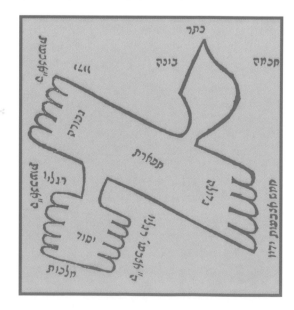

▶ THE 231 GATES
The 231 gates to ascendance are formed by the letters of the Hebrew alphabet and the 231 lines that link them. Alongside is the letter alef, drawn by the sixteenth-century Kabbalist Moses Cordovero. In contrast to the usual Tree of Life formation, here the individual letter is used to represent the ten sefirot, whose names are used as annotation.

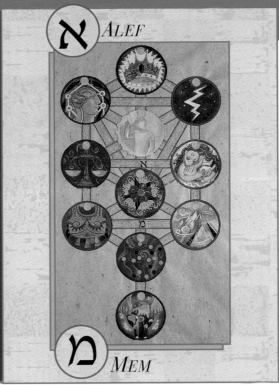

א ALEF

מ MEM

MEM מ

Mem is the thirteenth letter of the Hebrew alphabet and corresponds to *m* in English. It is a labial consonant, requiring the resonance of the voice between closed lips. According to the *Sefer Yetzirah*, God made *mem* king over water and subsequently formed the belly in the soul. *Mem* is associated with water, in Hebrew the word *mayim*, and resonates with the energy of emotion.

Mem is seen to span the path between the sefirot of Hod and Netzach, across the belly, which in the chakra system is the center of life-force energy (see pages 98–99). Much of our ego's sense of identity resides in these sefirot. The glory and splendor of human potential must be balanced against the desire to impress oneself on the world, leaving an enduring mark.

THE PATHS AND MODERN SCIENCE

The thirty-two paths on the Tree of Life may be linked with the human nervous system, as thirty-one nerves lead out from, and into the spinal cord. The thirty-second and highest path corresponds to the cranial nerves, which are twelve in number. As nerves are both receptors and effectors, carrying chemical messages along the sensory and motor neurons, so the paths function in a similar way. The practice of sacred geometry as found in Kabbalah may also be linked to quantum physics, as the equations of the letters and the paths can be seen as representations of the cosmic flow of quantum energy. It is certainly possible that the esoteric understanding of the Kabbalists over the centuries arrived at the same hypotheses or truths as today's astrophysicists.

▲ LIQUID OF LIFE
According to the Sefer Yetzirah, *the letter* mem *is king over water. Water links to the the world of Yetzirah, formation, and also represents emotion.*

THE PATH *to* UNITY

Consider the following questions as you look at the direction of your spirit:

✧ *What are some of the spiritual paths that you are walking in your life?*

✧ *Are these paths leading you toward or away from unity with Divine light and balance?*

✧ *Breathe the voiced aah and unvoiced breath of alef. How can this practice help you to balance your expressions of judgment/power and mercy/loving-kindness?*

✧ *Hum the sound mmm; this can help you balance your need for glory/splendor and enduring victory.*

THE SEVEN DOUBLES

The seven doubles are those Hebrew letters that can be pronounced in two ways: bet, gimel, dalet, khaf, pay, resh, *and* tav. *Isaac Luria assigned them to the seven vertical paths between the sefirot. Each of them, therefore, carries the energy of the Tree as well as connecting and channeling energy between the sefirot.*

PATHS OF THE THREE PILLARS

The central pillar of equilibrium is the route along which Divine light emanates downward from Keter and human aspirations ascend from Malkhut. The doubles that form this pillar are *dalet*, linking Keter and Tiferet, *resh*, from Tiferet to Yesod, and *tav*, leading from Yesod to Malkhut, which has only this individual path in the Lurianic system.

The three sefirot on the right pillar of mercy are connected by *bet*, linking Chokhmah and Chesed, and *khaf*, between Chesed and Netzach. Thus they focus and carry the expansive, outward-reaching energy.

On the left pillar of severity, the three sefirot are linked by *gimel*, between Binah and Gevurah, and *pay*, connnecting Gevurah and Hod. They therefore hold and transmit the receptive, restrictive energy of the left side.

THE SIGNIFICANT SEVEN

Another quality of the seven doubles is their dual nature. Chapter Four of the *Sefer Yetzirah* establishes their opposing qualities as good and bad. They are also linked to the seven known planets (the outer planets of Uranus, Neptune, and Pluto were only discovered during the past hundred years), associated with a day of the week and a direction one must face in order to transmit the associated qualities. It is worth noting that, over the centuries, Kabbalists have interpreted these associations differently, and it is possible that other variations may be found.

It is important to remember that the system envisioned by the Kabbalists is a five-dimensional one (*Sefer Yetzirah* 1:5). The practitioner must imagine standing inside a cube with three pairs of directions (up–down, east–west, north–south), while the other two dimensions move in time (beginning–end and good–evil). The student stands at the central position of the Moon (the psyche), looking toward the planets.

DALET

The fourth letter is *dalet* and has the numerical value 4. In Luria's system, it is the path between Keter and Tiferet. It is described as follows:

> *[God] made dalet king over seed and bound*
> *a crown to it*
> *And [God] combined this with that*
> *And with them formed the Sun*
> *in the universe,*
> *He formed the third day in the year*
> *and the right nostril of the soul, male and female.*
>
> SEFER YETZIRAH 4:10

Seven doubles: with them were engraved seven universes, seven firmaments, seven lands, seven seas, seven rivers, seven deserts, seven days, seven weeks, seven years, seven sabbaticals, seven jubilees, and the holy palace. Therefore God made sevens beloved under all the heavens.

SEFER YETZIRAH 4:15

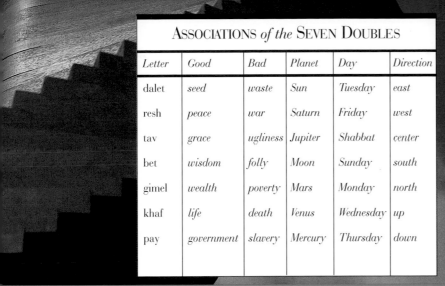

ASSOCIATIONS *of the* SEVEN DOUBLES

Letter	Good	Bad	Planet	Day	Direction
dalet	*seed*	*waste*	*Sun*	*Tuesday*	*east*
resh	*peace*	*war*	*Saturn*	*Friday*	*west*
tav	*grace*	*ugliness*	*Jupiter*	*Shabbat*	*center*
bet	*wisdom*	*folly*	*Moon*	*Sunday*	*south*
gimel	*wealth*	*poverty*	*Mars*	*Monday*	*north*
khaf	*life*	*death*	*Venus*	*Wednesday*	*up*
pay	*government*	*slavery*	*Mercury*	*Thursday*	*down*

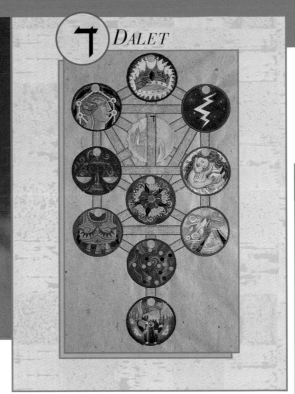

DALET

Dalet can be seen as a doorway between the blinding light emanating from Keter, and the beauty and potential within Tiferet (the Sun), the daughter of Chokhmah and Binah. It is interesting to note that another meaning of the same root word for *sun*, *chamah*, is *fury*, suggesting that the Divine radiance may blaze in anger as well as love. To meditate on it visualize a doorway, from the other side of which shines a brilliant white light. On your side of the doorway, imagine all the beauty and glory that can be part of the universe and your life. Consider what action you must take to facilitate the creation of this beauty.

THE PURPOSE OF THE PATHS

Abraham Abulafia opened the secrets of the Kabbalah in the thirteenth century by making meditative practices accessible. Part of his route to understanding consisted of learning different manipulations of the letters in order to benefit from the flow of energy represented by those combinations. One of his anonymous disciples explained his method in *Shaarei Tzedek* (Gates of Righteousness), published in 1295:

[The Kabbalistic way] consists of an amalgamation in the soul of man of the principles of mathematical and of natural science, after he has first studied the literal meanings of the Torah and the faith ... to train his mind and not in the manner of a simpleton to believe in everything ... For the prophet would impart to us the secrets of the combinations of consonants and of ... vowels between them, the paths by which the secret and active powers emanate, and the reason that this emanation is sometimes hindered from above."

ANON

▲ SEVEN DOUBLES
The vertical lines of the seven doubles link the sefirot and afford paths of ascent. This concept may be experienced through towering sculptures or buildings, which can also lift the spirit in several dimensions.

MEDITATING *on the* PATH *of* DALET

Consider the following questions as you look at the direction of your spirit:

✡ *As you face the east and the rising of the sun, ask yourself what seeds you have planted and what waste you have created.*

✡ *What can you do to ensure that your actions will bring growth rather than be wasteful or destructive?*

✡ *Once you have decided what needs to be done, resolve to begin on Tuesday.*

RESH *and* TAV

Resh and tav *are respectively the twentieth and twenty-second letters of the Hebrew alphabet. Along with* dalet, *they are the paths on the middle pillar of equilibrium and thus connect the central sefirot, creating a two-way flow of balancing energy between above and below.*

RESH ר

Resh is pronounced like *r* and has a numerical value of 200. Its symbolic meaning is the head, which in Hebrew is *rosh*. It is the path connecting Tiferet and Yesod, Beauty and Foundation.

   Resh is set over peace and war, and *Shabbatai*, the Hebrew word for Saturn, is derived from the same root as *Shabbat*, the seventh day of rest, which begins on Friday evening. *Resh* connects Tiferet and Yesod, the path between the grace and beauty of the Sun and the fundamental identity and psyche of the Moon. In the world of Yetzirah, this is the link between the identity of self and the feeling ego. It may be interpreted as the path connecting what goes on in the heart and head of a person trying to make sense of who he or she is. The genitals are the part of the body associated with Yesod, and these are connected by the path to the solar plexus of Tiferet. In the chakra system these parallel the primal physical identity of the root chakra and the intellectual identity of the solar plexus chakra.

▶ HEAD
The head is a key theme in Jewish mythology and is used in many spiritual and linguistic contexts.

> [God] made the letter resh king over peace and bound a crown to it. And [God] combined this with that and with them formed Saturn in the universe, Friday in the year, the left nostril in the soul, male and female.
>
> SEFER YETZIRAH 4:13

MEDITATING *on the* PATH *of* RESH

Imagine the path of resh in your head and your heart:

✡ *Consider how much of your life you spend at peace with yourself and the world, and how much in a state of warlike destructiveness.*

✡ *To rebalance the energy, sit down on Friday and allow the beauty and glory of Tiferet to enter your heart and head. Imagine yourself calm and without any need to wage war or win conflicts.*

✡ *You may wish to play the "Saturn" movement from Gustav Holst's suite The Planets, and allow the energy to flow over you.*

✡ *What must you do to bring peace into your essential self, your life, and the world around you?*

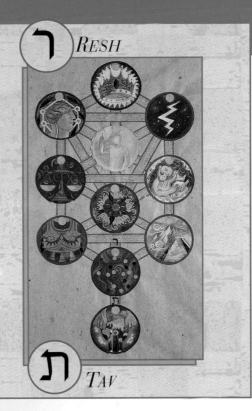

RESH

TAV

TAV ת

Tav is the last letter of the alphabet, with the primary sound *t*. It has a numerical value of 400, and the symbolic meaning of the letter is a cross. *Tav* is the path between Yesod and Malkhut, linking the fundamental identity of the self with the earthly realm of the Shekhinah, where all human activity takes place.

ESSENTIAL LINKS

With the opposing qualities of grace and ugliness, *tav* mediates between the descending manifestation of Divine grace and beauty in the world, and the ugliness that humanity creates by turning away from the Divine light. *Tav* links the emotional self of Yesod with the physical self of the body. It is described as forming Jupiter, whose Hebrew name *tzedek* also means *righteousness*. Thus the largest planet, Jupiter, exerts the force of righteousness—which humanity can receive and express in the world, or ignore at its peril.

▲ SATURN'S RINGS
The exquisite equilibrium of Saturn's rings symbolizes the dynamic equilibrium between the Sun of Tiferet and the Moon of Yesod, which are the sefirot associated with this path.

MEDITATING *on the* PATH *of* TAV

For the path of tav, *consider your body and your ego:*

✿ *Give yourself time and space on the Sabbath to rest and consider what lies at the center of your life.*

✿ *Do you respect your body and care for it by taking exercise and eating healthily?*

✿ *What do you do, in moments of weakness, that creates ugliness in the world, and how can you desist from those actions?*

✿ *Visualize your life as filled with grace, and imagine what you need to do to enable that vision to become reality.*

BET *and* GIMEL

Bet and gimel *are the second and third letters of the alphabet and occupy the corresponding positions on the right and left pillars, that is, linking the highest to the middle sefirot on each column. They also represent the first and second days of the week, Sunday and Monday, and the opposing directions south and north.*

▼ PATH DIRECTIONS
The paths of bet *and* gimel *are associated with the opposing compass directions of south and north.*

BET ב

Bet, the second letter corresponding to *b*, is also sometimes pronounced *v*. It has a numerical value of 2 and its symbolic meaning is a house, in Hebrew *bayit*. *Bet* is the first letter in the Torah, the beginning of the word *bereshit*, meaning *in the beginning*. Thus this letter is about first principles. *Bet* is the vertical path linking Chokhmah and Chesed. Chokhmah is the wisdom that is required to build a house that will stand firm and provide for its inhabitants. Likewise, Chesed is the mercy and love that enable us to dwell in God's house and with others in our actual homes.

The word used for moon, *l'vanah*, is uncommon, used only in the love poetry of *Song of Songs* 6:10, "Who is she ... fair as the moon, clear as the sun ..." and in Isaiah 30:26, where God's

promise of redemption states that "the light of the moon shall be like the light of the sun, and the light of the sun shall be sevenfold ..." These two comparisons suggest that the energy of *bet* contains the potential for transformation and growth, from a lightless reflective surface to a fair beauty shining with its own inherent brightness.

With the dual qualities of wisdom and folly, *bet* carries the energy of Chokhmah down the pillar of mercy toward humanity, where it can be expressed in action. It also reminds us that turning away from the wisdom available to us can lead to folly.

MEDITATING *on the* PATH *of* BET

Access the path of bet *through these four exercises:*

✡ *Choose a peaceful Sunday and find an undisturbed spot.*

✡ *Consider the wisdom that has come to you from teachers, friends, and the circumstances of your life.*

✡ *Focus on ways in which you can express that wisdom toward others as loving-kindness and for the repair of the world.*

✡ *Put your ideas into practice at once.*

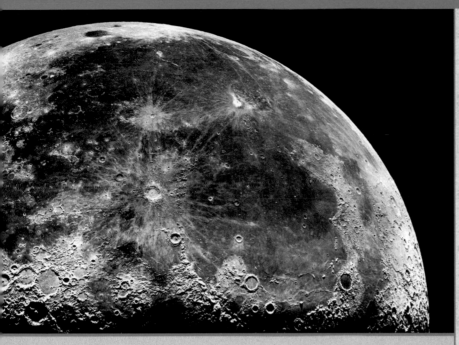

ב BET

GIMEL ג

GIMEL ג

Gimel, the third letter of the alphabet, has the numerical value of 3 and a hard pronunciation of *g*. Its symbolic meaning is a camel, in Hebrew *gamal*, and has the associations of the desert and the ability to hold and endure. Set opposite *bet*, on the pillar of severity, *gimel* is the vertical path between Binah and Gevurah, linking the energies of understanding and judgment.

The *Sefer Yetzirah* indicates that each letter can be used to influence a part of the body. Similarly, the associated day is auspicious for the energy of the path. Thus Monday would be a good day on which to initiate action directed toward creating or increasing wealth.

Linking Binah to Gevurah, the path of *bet* can help to develop the understanding of Binah to be expressed as wise judgment and proper use of power. It can help to check any tendency toward excess, which might lead to harm or poverty.

▲ THE MOON

The Moon, feminine symbol of mystery and emotion, is the heavenly body created by God from the letter bet.

▲ DESERT CARRIER

The word camel *comes from the Hebrew word,* gamal, *formed from the letter* gimel. *Just as the path of gimel carries the knowledge of the sefirah of Binah to the judgment of Gevurah, so the camel carries the traveler through the wilderness.*

MEDITATING *on the* PATH *of* GIMEL

Use these exercises to help you consider the associations of gimel:

✿ *Take time on Monday to sit quietly where you will be undisturbed.*

✿ *Consider how you use the knowledge and understanding that you have. You may want to focus on a particular issue to resolve a problem or guide your actions.*

✿ *Do you use your power and judgment to the detriment of others when you attempt to increase your personal wealth or power?*

✿ *Decide on a change of attitude or a course of action that comes from a willingness to share rather than to take from others. Put it into practice at once.*

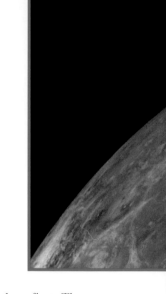

KHAF and PAY

Khaf, *pronounced* kh, *is the middle of the Hebrew alphabet and its numerical value is 20. Its secondary pronunciation is* k, *and its symbolic meaning is an open palm, indicated by the shape of the letter.* Khaf *links the sefirot of Chesed and Netzach, forming a two-way channel for the flow of mercy and enduring victory.*

▲ THE PLANET OF *PAY*
The word for Mercury is kokhav *in Hebrew, meaning* star. *Although the smallest planet, it is also the hottest.*

KHAF כ

Venus, the planet associated with the sefirah of Netzach, is here called *nogah* in Hebrew, which means *brightness*. As the brightest planet in the heavens, it symbolizes light. *Khaf*'s dual qualities are life and death, and the energy that flows between Chesed and Netzach can lead either way. In meditations, it is suggested that the soft pronunciation of the letters helps to attain the positive qualities, while the hard pronunciation influences the negative ones. Thus the sound *khaf* is used to focus on life, and *kaf* on death.

PAY פ

Pay, pronounced *p*, with its soft sound of *f*, is a double letter in two senses. Like *khaf*, it has a different form when it is the final letter of a word. Its numerical value is 80 and its symbolic meaning is the mouth. The Hebrew word for *mouth* is *pay*, and it is the first letter of the word *pardes*, meaning *orchard* or *paradise*, which has great symbolic significance in Kabbalah. It is the last of the double letters.

The connecting path of *pay* is a channel for the powerful energy of the judgment and strength of Gevurah and the glory and splendor of Hod. *Pay*'s qualities of dominion, or government, and slavery are clearly con-

nected to the energy of the sefirot. The proper use of power and splendor is to do the Divine will, and an excess of zeal for personal power or grandeur will result in some kind of enslavement, either of the self or of others. Mercury, the planet made from *pay*, is formed from the same root as the Hebrew word for *star*.

> *[God] made the letter* khaf *king over life and bound a crown to it and combined this one with that one and formed with them Venus in the universe, Wednesday in the year, the left eye in the soul, male and female.*
>
> SEFER YETZIRAH *4:10*

MEDITATING *on the* PATH *of* KHAF

Imagine the path of* khaf *in your head and your heart:

✡ *Sit out on a Wednesday evening, when Venus is setting, and look up at the planet that looks like a star.*

✡ *Focus on your life up to now and consider what you wish to be the enduring qualities and achievements that you will leave behind. Remember that what endures may be those things that share your talents with others.*

✡ *Think about what you can give to life, rather than take from it.*

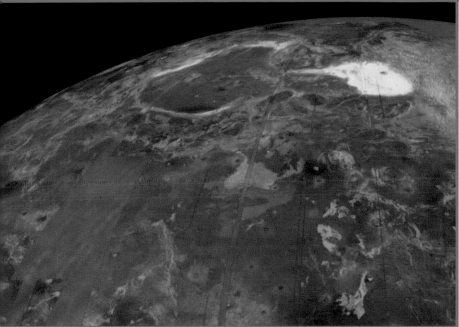

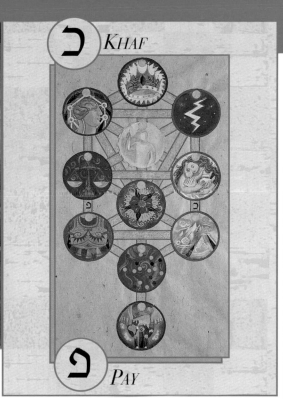

ך KHAF

פ PAY

A FINAL WORD ON THE DOUBLE LETTERS

From each of the doubles is formed an orifice in the head: the left and right nostrils (*resh* and *dalet*), the left and right eye (*khaf* and *bet*), the left and right ear (*pay* and *gimel*) and the mouth (*tav*). These openings are our sensory organs, the channels through which we take in our sense of the world. Kabbalah offers, through these paths, an opportunity to sharpen our senses and use them more effectively for good. For just as we take in information, so we have the choice to be responsible for how we pass it on.

▲ VENUS

This image of Venus demonstrates the intrinsic beauty of the planet. Created from the letter khaf, *the Hebrew name for Venus is* Nogah, *meaning brightness.*

◄ PLACE OF PRAYER

The beautiful interior of West London Synagogue exemplifies the purpose of religious art, to glorify God and help the spirit ascend in its journey toward yichud, *oneness with the Divine.*

MEDITATING *on the* PATH *of* PAY

Imagine the path of pay *with these simple exercises:*

✡ *Choose Thursday, the day associated with* pay, *to have some quiet time alone outdoors at night. If possible, check an astronomical map to find Mercury.*

✡ *Look up at the stars and try to locate Mercury. Alternatively, just contemplate the stars and then look down at the Earth.*

✡ *Think about the ways you dominate others and the Earth, and to what extent you enslave others, or are enslaved, by the patterns of your life.*

✡ *Allow yourself to consider how you might change the way you relate to others in terms of power and glory. Perhaps you need to strengthen your assertiveness or to learn to be more submissive.*

✡ *Choose one relationship in which a change of energy will improve both the relationship and the world. Commit to making that change and put it into practice.*

THE TWELVE ELEMENTALS

The twelve elemental paths are the letters hay, vav, zayin, chet, tet, yod, lamed, nun, samech, ayin, tzadi, kuf. *Their foundation is speech, thought, motion, sight, hearing, action, coition, smell, sleep, anger, taste, and laughter. These letters comprise the diagonal paths between sefirot on the Tree—they are known as elementals, or simples, because they have only one pronunciation.*

ASSOCIATIONS OF THE TWELVE ELEMENTALS

Letter	Value	Symbol	Foundation	Boundary	Constellation	Hebrew Month	Organ
hay	5	window	speech	east upper	Aries	Nissan	right foot
vav	6	hook	thought	east northern	Taurus	Iyyar	right kidney
zayin	7	weapon	motion	east lower	Gemini	Sivan	left foot
chet	8	fence	sight	south upper	Cancer	Tammuz	right hand
tet	9	serpent	hearing	south eastern	Leo	Av	left kidney
yod	10	hand	action	south lower	Virgo	Elul	left hand
lamed	30	ox-goad	coition	west upper	Libra	Tishrei	gallbladder
nun	50	fish	smell	west southern	Scorpio	Cheshvan	intestine
samech	60	prop	sleep	west lower	Sagittarius	Kislev	kivah (ruminant 4th stomach)
ayin	70	eye	anger	north upper	Capricorn	Tevet	liver
tzadi	90	fishhook	taste	north western	Aquarius	Shevat	korkeban (gizzard)
kuf	100	back of head	laughter	north lower	Pisces	Adar	spleen

To understand the complexity of the Kabbalists' vision, it is helpful to view the multidimensional universe as a cube with temporal and spatial dimensions. As mentioned earlier, the descriptions in the *Sefer Yetzirah* have been variously interpreted over the centuries. The cubic structure was established by the extraordinary eighteenth-century Kabbalist Eliahu ben Shlomo, the Gaon of Vilna, known as the Gra.

According to Aryeh Kaplan, these twelve elemental letters are connected to the twelve tribes of Israel, thus establishing a historical relationship

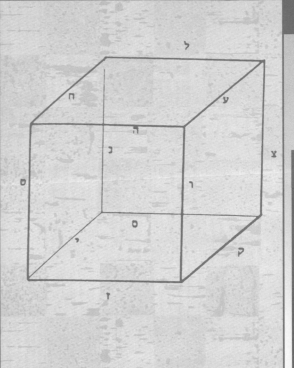

The twelve elementals

Their foundation is the twelve

diagonal boundaries

They extend continually until

eternity of eternities

And it is they that are the

boundaries of the universe.

SEFER YETZIRAH 5:2

THE ELEMENTALS AND THE ZODIAC

For the scholars of Kabbalah, astrological patterns and an understanding of the influence of the movements of stars and planets were an inherent part of their cosmology. In the commentary of Abraham ben David, known as the Raavad (1120–1198 C.E.), there is a schema linking all the associations of twelve connected to the elemental letters: the permutations of the tetragrammaton, the foundations (or houses), the tribes of Israel, the months, and the signs of the zodiac. As the schema appears in a sixteenth-century edition, it is likely that its author is in fact a later Kabbalist, Yosef ha-Arukh, Joseph the Tall, who lived in the fourteenth century.

The Kabbalists developed a very complex mathematical system involving the time of birth and the numerical value of the person's Hebrew name and that of his or her mother. The zodiac signs are associated with the lunar months, rather than with the sun signs of Western astrology. The constellations are channels of Divine energy from the stars to the world of humanity.

▲ NEW DIMENSIONS
Just as the radio telescope searches out the boundaries of space, so the twelve elementals define the boundaries of the Kabbalistic universe. The multi-dimensional cube is envisioned with three pairs of geographic directions: up–down, east–west, and north–south, and two pairs of time dimensions: beginning–end and good–evil.

with geographical boundaries, as the camp positions of the tribes were established in the Torah (Numbers 1–2). Additionally, *Sefer ha-Bahir* (95) says that inside the boundaries of the twelve elementals is the Tree of Life. The twelve elemental letters hold the energy of the diagonal paths between the sefirot. Thus they frame the parameters of the metaphysical universe and our physical and spiritual reality.

HAY *and* VAV

Hay and vav *are the fifth and sixth letters of the Hebrew alphabet and, with* yod, *form the tetragrammaton YHVH. They also form part of the verb* to be *and connect at a linguistic level to existence and God.* Hay *also means the definite article* the, *while* vav *is the conjunction* and, *connecting nouns and verbs, people, and actions. The complex structure of the language confirms the view that the letters contain powerful energies from higher realms.*

HAY ה

Hay is the diagonal path that leads from Keter, at the top of the Tree of Life, to Chokhmah, the second sefirah. It is the path that channels the lightning flash of Divine emanation along the first step of its journey through the sefirot to the realm of Malkhut and human life. It also carries the energy of the uniqueness and unity of God. In the other direction, it directs the ascent of spirit from wisdom to the Divine crown and source of light. The pictorial symbol of the letter is a window, and *hay* can be viewed as a window to the Divine brilliance of God. Only the most righteous and perfect human beings are deemed capable of attaining this level of spiritual ascent toward unification.

Hay, ruler over speech, forms the constellation Aries (*taleh* in Hebrew, meaning *lamb*) and is the first of the signs of the zodiac, corresponding to Nissan, the first month of the lunar year. It suggests that this month in the spring is an auspicious time to direct attention to the work of unification and to begin any project or activity that relates to speech.

[God] made the letter hay *king over speech and bound a crown to it And combined this one and that one and with them [God] formed Aries in the universe, Nissan in the year, and the right foot in the soul, male and female.*

SEFER YETZIRAH 5:7

MEDITATING *on the* PATH *of* HAY

Consider the attributes of the letter* hay *as you try these exercises:

✿ *Look upward toward the east, ideally as the sun rises.*

✿ *As you welcome the warming energy of the sun, give thanks for your life and another day.*

✿ *Consider how you will use your power of speech today. What restrictions must you take to ensure that your speech causes no harm? What generosity must you express to ensure that your speech is beneficial?*

✿ *Hay guides you with the highest wisdom toward the light of understanding. Let yourself seek that wisdom.*

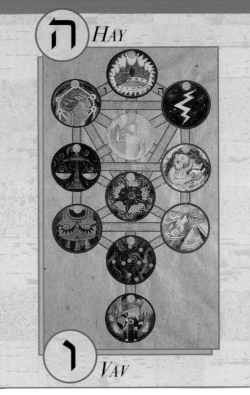

ה *HAY*

ו *VAV*

VAV ו

[God] made the letter vav *king over thought and*

bound a crown to it

And combined this one with that one and with them

[God] formed Taurus in the universe,

Iyyar in the year

and the right kidney in the soul, male and female.

SEFER YETZIRAH 5:7

Vav, the sixth letter, is the path from Keter to Binah, and the counterpart of *hay*. With *hay* and the mother letter *shin*, it forms the first triad of the Tree of Life and holds the highest energy of ascent. The path between the two sefirot channels the Divine energy to inspire the acquisition of knowledge. The letter *vav* represents the spine and can be seen as the pillar that carries our nerve impulses. Thus it is a conduit for all that we learn.

Vav forms the zodiac sign of Taurus (in Hebrew *shor*, or ox) and oversees the spring month of Iyyar. It is a time between the festival of Pesach (Passover), which celebrates the liberation from Egyptian slavery under the leadership of Moses, and the festival of Shavuot (Pentecost), which is seven weeks later. This latter holiday celebrates the first harvest and the giving of the Torah to the Israelites at Mount Sinai.

▲ ARIES, THE RAM

Aries is the first sign of the zodiac, formed by the Hebrew letter hay. *This path brings Divine light from the sefirah of Keter to the wisdom of Chokhmah.*

MEDITATING *on the* PATH *of* VAV

Take time to visualize the path associated with the Hebrew letter vav:

✡ *Visualize your spine and feel its strength. Allow yourself to bend and weave to experience its flexibility.*

✡ *Now imagine both your spine and the letter* vav *as a conduit of Divine light and energy. Imagine that light entering your soul and your brain.*

✡ *Feel the warmth and love and the flowering of understanding that come with being receptive to God's light and love.*

✡ *Remember that Iyyar (usually the month of May) is a time to consolidate your intellectual powers. Consider how you can strengthen your thought processes.*

ZAYIN *and* KUF

Zayin, with a numerical value of 7, plays a vital role in bringing the energies of the higher sefirot down into the lower seven. Kuf is the path corresponding to zayin, the diagonal linking Binah and Chesed. Its numerical value is 100 and it is therefore the highest of the elementals. These two paths cross the mystical non-sefirah of Da'at, and are crucial in transferring the higher energies.

ZAYIN

Zayin links Chokhmah, revelatory wisdom, and Gevurah, strength and judgment. Its symbol, slightly resembling a sword, gives it a symbolic meaning as a weapon.

Overseeing motion, *zayin* also forms the left foot. In psychobiological terms, the left side of the body is ruled by the right, lateral, nonrational, and generally nondominant side of the brain (unless you are left-handed). Thus when you stride forward with the left foot, your step is guided by the energy of Chokhmah. You can use that wisdom to exercise careful judgment in your actions and your steps.

Gemini is the astrological sign of *zayin*, and the Hebrew word *t'omim* means *twins*. The word is used to describe the struggling twins Jacob and Esau in Rebeccah's womb (Genesis 25:24) and the twin sons of Tamar (Genesis 38:27). The dual nature of twins, identical and yet struggling for individual recognition and power, connects with the energy of Gevurah. More relevant to Kabbalistic interpretation is the use of the word in *Song of Songs*, comparing the two breasts of the writer's beloved to the twin fawns of a gazelle (7:3–4). The love imagery is taken to mean, on its highest level, the exquisite beauty of the Shekhinah, beloved feminine aspect of God in Malkhut.

[God] made the letter zayin *ruler*
over motion and bound a crown to it
And combined this one and that
one and with them [God] formed
Gemini in the universe,
Sivan in the year
And the left foot in the soul,
male and female.

SEFER YETZIRAH 5:7

MEDITATING *on the* PATH *of* ZAYIN

***Take time out to think deeply about the path of* zayin.**

✡ *Stand on your left foot and balance for a moment or two. Be aware of how it feels to stand this way.*

✡ *Walk for a few moments, concentrating on leading with your left foot. Then change to leading with your right foot (hay) and notice any differences.*

✡ *As you continue to walk, consider the two sides of your nature, what you consider to be your strengths and weaknesses. Think about how you can acknowledge all of these qualities as parts of yourself.*

✡ *How do your strength and the exercising of judgment influence the growth of wisdom in your life? To what extent do you allow the wisdom that comes to you to apply to your actions and judgments?*

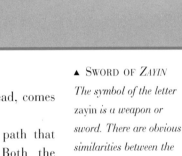

KUF

The symbol for *kuf*, the back of the head, comes from its distinctive shape.

Between Binah and Chesed is the path that brings understanding into action. Both the instinctive knowing that comes from Chokhmah and the rational knowledge that is the result of experience and learning lead to the expression of mercy and loving-kindness in the world. Empathy and sympathy enable us to relate to the needs of others and to reach out and offer love and mercy to them.

Similarly, the love and understanding we receive from others can enhance our own understanding of what it is to be a human being. The more we give and receive love, the more we understand that love and oneness are fundamental to our human spirit.

With laughter as the human expression of *kuf*, linked to the month of Adar, this path was seen by the rabbis as crucial to the understanding of the festival of Purim (Lots), which takes place on the full moon of Adar. Purim celebrates the survival of the Jews of Persia in the face of a plot to exterminate them. Told in the Book of Esther, it is a story full of apparent coincidence in which the name of God is never mentioned. Yet the invisible hand of God can be felt at every point in the story. So too with the path of *kuf*: the invisible will and knowledge of God (Da'at) underlie the path between Binah and Chesed.

▲ SWORD OF *ZAYIN*
The symbol of the letter zayin is a weapon or sword. There are obvious similarities between the letter and its meaning.

MEDITATING *on the* PATH *of* KUF

Imagine the path of kuf *in your head and heart:*

✡ *Think about everything you have learned since you began your exploration of Kabbalah. Where has your understanding come from?*

✡ *Why do you think you have the power of intellect, which enables you to confront new concepts and grasp their meaning and relevance?*

✡ *How can you use your knowledge to extend loving-kindness to others?*

✡ *Consider that the love offered to you by others is a gift.*

Tet, Yod, Lamed, and Nun

Tet and yod *are the corresponding paths that form the triad of Netzach, Hod, and Tiferet.* Tet *is the ninth letter of the alphabet, with a value of 9.* Yod *is the tenth letter, with a value of 10.* Lamed *and* nun *form the two diagonal paths opposite* tet *and* yod. Lamed *links Hod (Splendor) to Yesod (Foundation), while* nun *runs between Netzach (Enduring Victory) and Yesod.*

Tet ט and Yod י

The symbolic meaning of *tet* is a serpent, forming a circle with the tail almost entering the mouth. *Tet* links Tiferet (Beauty) and Hod (Splendor) and is therefore the path that brings Divine beauty into existence as the glory and splendor of creation. *Tet* enables us to appreciate how all the wonderful things that we see and experience are an expression of God's glory.

Yod is the first letter of the tetragrammaton and thus has an explicit connection with the Divine name. It is the path between Tiferet and Netzach, bringing beauty, which is the daughter of Chokhmah and Binah, into the world as an expression of endurance and victory. The mountains that tower over the land, the icebergs that float majestically on the seas, the life processes that maintain the ecological system, are all expressions of Netzach empowered by Tiferet.

Hearing and action are their two qualities, which remind us of the importance of the senses in appreciating what we do and what others do. All the paths converge at Tiferet, and from that magnificent center comes the possibility of creating forms and actions that bring Divine attributes into our human reality.

Lamed ל and Nun נ

Together *lamed* and *nun* form a diamond bisected by the mother letter *mem*. *Lamed* looks like its symbolic meaning, an ox-goad, a curved stick used to prod the animal in its work. Linking Hod and Yesod, *lamed* carries the higher energy down into the realm of the self, where distinctive acts of creativity and self-expression occur. It rules over sexual intercourse, the fundamental human act of expressing life force, love, and creativity. As Libra, the scales, *lamed* indicates the obligation to balance the needs of the ego for self-expression and the restriction of self that is necessary to glorify God.

The scales of Libra meld with the festivals of Tishrei, the High Holy Days, also called the Days of Awe. During this period every Jew is required to balance the actions of his or her own life over the previous year, to do "an accounting of the soul." Between the New Year, Rosh Hashanah, and the Day of Atonement, Yom Kippur, everyone has an opportunity to seek and grant forgiveness for wrong actions done to or by others and to make peace with God.

Nun has the symbol of a fish and forms the zodiac sign of Scorpio and the month of Cheshvan

[God] made the letter tet *king over hearing and bound a crown to it And combined this one with that one and with them [God] formed Leo in the universe, Av in the year, and the left kidney in the soul, male and female.*

[God] made the letter yod *king over action and bound a crown to it And combined this one with that one and with them [God] formed Virgo in the universe, Elul in the year And the left hand in the soul, male and female.*

SEFER YETZIRAH 5:8

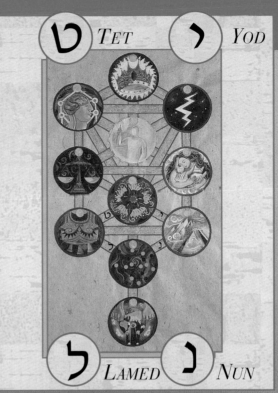

ט TET	י YOD
ל LAMED	נ NUN

▼ SERPENT OF *TET*

Tet *represents the serpent and links the sefirot of Tiferet (Beauty) and Hod (Splendor). In other cultural traditions, the circular serpent is used as an image of eternity.*

(October/November). This is a time of consolidation after the four major festivals in the preceding month of Tishrei. The darkness begins to draw in, and the self must find ways of preparing for winter, the dark time of the year. There are no Jewish festivals during this month, which indicates that a great deal of personal work needs to be done while there is no other external distraction of religious and communal celebration.

The path between Netzach and Yesod is one of expression of the self in the world, making a mark, and being influenced by those things in life that are enduring. With "the intestine in the soul" comes the work of assimilation. As the process of digestion moves from the breaking down of material in the stomach to the absorption in the intestine, so the soul can use this time to absorb the energy that descends from the higher sefirot, in preparation for work to be done.

SAMECH, AYIN, TZADI, and CHET

Samech and ayin *form the paths that lead from the higher sefirot to Tiferet.* Samech *is the path between Chokhmah and Tiferet, while* ayin *links Binah and Tiferet. The two energies relate to the mind of God and its manifestation in beauty. The letters* tzadi *and* chet *are the last of the elementals, linking Gevurah and Tiferet from the left pillar, and Chesed and Tiferet from the right.*

SAMECH ס AND AYIN ע

Samech forms the sign of Sagittarius, the archer. The Hebrew word is *keshet*, meaning *bow*, both the bow of the archer and the rainbow set in the sky by God after the Flood, a sign of his promise never to destroy the world again in that way. Both the archer's bow and the rainbow are expressions of grace, beauty, and the physical laws in action. The energy of *samech* therefore carries Divine wisdom into creative expression.

Ayin, linking Binah to Tiferet, carries the energy of understanding that comes from God, which is manifested in beauty. With *samech*, these two aspects of God's mind coalesce in Tiferet, in the exquisite beauty of creation. *Ayin* is ruler over anger and reminds us that God's understanding, on the left pillar of severity, may lead to expression of anger as well as love. Linked to the liver, which is the organ of processing many life functions, *ayin* indicates that this path supervises the processing of thought that must be undertaken.

[God] made the letter samech *king over sleep and bound a crown to it*

And combined this one with that one and with them [God] formed

Sagittarius in the universe, Kislev in the year

And the kivah *[fourth stomach of ruminant] in the soul, male and female.*

SEFER YETZIRAH 5:9

MEDITATING *on the* PATH *of* SAMECH

Imagine the path of* samech *in your head and your heart:

✡ *Focus on the cold and darkness of winter, with its short days and long nights. During that time, it is possible to cease from busy-ness and contemplate how the wisdom of the universe descends from the infinity of space and time.*

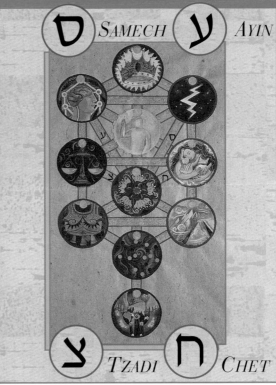

Within the image 3:

ס SAMECH   ע AYIN

צ TZADI   ח CHET

TZADI צ AND CHET ח

Luria's system shifts the position of *chet* and *kuf* from its alphabetical and chronological sequence. However, in some systems *chet* is seen as the path linking Keter through Da'at to Tiferet, while *kuf* connects Netzach to Yesod. The Gra, Eliahu ben Shlomo, placed *tzadi* between Netzach and Malkhut and *chet* between Binah and Tiferet.

Tzadi's symbolic meaning is a fishhook and it forms the sign of Aquarius, the water carrier. *Tzadi*, ruler over taste, brings another sense into the manifestation of beauty in Tiferet. *Chet*, which oversees sight, carries a further sense. Tiferet, at the center, receives the energies of sleep, anger, hearing, action, taste, and sight.

As ruler over sight, *chet* enables the student to relate the beauty of Tiferet and the love of Chesed to the whole world. Through sight we receive images of the world, which our brain names, explains, and adapts. Thus the path of *chet* offers us an opportunity to see more clearly what the Divine will create for us.

▲ MYSTIC FISHHOOK
The letter tzadi *is usually associated with a fish-hook. The angular formation of the letter shows obvious similarities with the hook, as its essential qualities have remained the same since the dawn of humanity.*

MEDITATING *on the* PATH *of* CHET

Take time to think about the path of chet:

✿ *Look at your right hand, the organ formed by* chet. *Think about all the things you do with your right hand, and what life might be like without it. Consider how much love and beauty you could bring into the world through the use of your right hand.*

✿ *Gaze around you and try to look intently at the things you normally take for granted. Realize that your sight enables you to appreciate the beauty that resides in everything, and commit yourself to taking the time to see with more clarity and appreciation.*

THE POWER OF ANGELS

► JUST LIKE US
Acting as intermediaries between the upper and lower worlds, angels may be messengers who appear no different from anyone else. This angelic representation is taken from the classic 1946 movie, A Matter of Life and Death.

The world of Kabbalah takes for granted the existence of angels, who interact with humanity in the lower worlds, and archangels, who populate the world of Beriah (Creation) and their sefirot. The English word angel *comes from the Greek and Latin* angelus, *a translation of the Hebrew word* malakh, *which means* messenger.

Throughout the centuries, the concept of angels changed from beings in the court of the Almighty who acted as go-betweens in the world of humanity, to a Christian image of beings expressing God's grace and judgment.

ANGELS PAST *and* PRESENT

Angelic myths arose in ancient Persia and became part of Jewish mystical tradition during the Babylonian exile (586–536 B.C.E.). Through the Talmudic period (ca. 200 B.C.E.–500 C.E.) some rabbis used angels in their explanations of biblical texts to represent Divine will and judgment. They were seen as supernal beings with an independent existence, but also subject to the rule of God.

> *God's dwelling place is in the seventh heaven,*
> *next to which is the abode of the pious;*
> *and the angels rank after the latter.*
>
> TALMUD ROSH HASHANAH 24B

▲ THE CHERUB'S ROLE
The cherubim appear all through the Bible, from Adam and Eve through to the building of the Ark of the Covenant, where they were to be created out of gold to sit at either end of the Ark with their wings outspread. They came to be portrayed in Christian art as lovable babies.

ANGELS PASSING BY

Let these questions help you see people in a new light:

✡ *What do you imagine an angel to be?*

✡ *Do you notice the people who cross your path in life?*

✡ *Have you ever had an encounter with a stranger that seemed beyond the ordinary?*

ORIGIN AND HIERARCHY

Angels are rarely identified in the later biblical writings, except for the books of Ezekiel, Zechariah, and Daniel, where they abound. Early Kabbalists developed the concept of biblical angels; the *Zohar* and *Sefer Yetzirah* linked them to the four elements, the sefirot, and gave them a hierarchy.

The angelic population in Kabbalah is almost limitless. The *Zohar* (2:42b) describes how "God created beings to minister to the holy vessels: one throne supported by four columns, with six steps leading to the throne; ten in all ... God prepared angelic hierarchies for the throne to serve Him." In the *Hekhalot* (Halls) texts (first century C.E.), each angel is ascribed to one of the seven heavenly halls in the palaces in Eden where souls go after death. Kabbalists developed various practices to ascend to these sacred halls.

The *Sefer Yetzirah* claims angels were created from fire in the sefirah of Binah (Understanding) in the world of Beriah (Creation). The serafim are the highest order who surrounded the Throne of Glory. The word *serafim* comes from the Hebrew *saraf*, meaning *to burn*, so it is easy to see how they became associated with light.

The chayyot angels, or "living creatures,"

◄ GLORY AND LIGHT
*The highest archangel
Metatron, Prince of the
Presence, protects the
Divine throne. Fire
surrounds the angel,
representing the spirit.*

◄ THE TRAVEL OF
ANGELS
*Jacob dreamed of a
stairway carrying angels
between heaven and
Earth.*

inhabit Yetzirah (Formation) and the six sefirot below Binah. These are the angels Ezekiel saw in his vision of the Merkavah, or chariot (Ezekiel 1); this story became a key source of mystic interpretation. In the sefirah of Malkhut (Kingdom) live the ophanim, the wheel-like angels of the world of Assiyah (Action), who appear to human beings.

JACOB: EMBODIMENT OF TIFERET

Two powerful angelic narratives in the Bible are Jacob's dream (Genesis 28:10–22) and his wrestling with the angel (Genesis 32:2–33). In the first, Jacob dreamed of a stairway stretching to heaven, with angels moving up and down it. This dream was used to explain angelic travel between the worlds of Beriah (Creation) and Yetzirah (Formation) and the earthly world of Malkhut (Kingdom). The dream has become an expression of the cosmic link between heaven and Earth and the potential for human ascent.

Years later, Jacob met an angel by a river while on his way to seek reconciliation with his brother Esau. They wrestled until dawn, and Jacob won. The angel renamed him Israel, one who wrestles with God, as a symbol of the experience that transformed him. This struggle became a symbol of tensions between the forces of light and dark, and the river, as in later Greek and Roman mythology, symbolized the challenge of overcoming hazards, as Jacob later became the father of the Israelites.

Jacob also became the symbol of Tiferet (Beauty) because he balanced the opposing sefirot Gevurah (Judgment) and Chesed (Mercy).

WHO ARE *the* ANGELS?

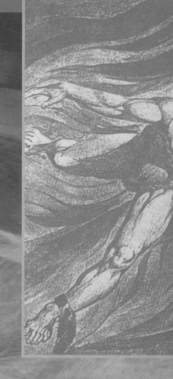

Angels are individuals, each with his own task and able to function only in his allotted sphere. They are dispatched daily down to the sefirah of Malkhut (Kingdom) to serve either the human body or soul. Some are ministering angels, moving up and down the right pillar of mercy; others are corrupting angels, moving on the left pillar of severity and judgment on the Tree of Life. Some of these angels also exercise Divine punishment on Earth.

In Kabbalah, most angels are concerned with judgment; they are endowed with wings and are of varying size. Sandalphon, for example, is said to be taller than his fellows by the length of a five-hundred-year journey, marking an intriguing interplay between time and space long before contemporary ideas of space and time. Although practical Kabbalists tried to use angelic names to overturn their destiny, theoretical Kabbalists thought humanity, as the apex of God's Creation, was ranked above the angels.

CHANGING NAMES

Angels have many names in the Old Testament. In Genesis 18, they are the *men* who visit Sarah and Abraham; in Genesis 19, they are *messengers*, who save Lot; and in Genesis 21, they are *elohim* (meaning *beings of God*), who save Hagar and Ishmael. Most potently, they are *malakh YHVH*, or *messengers of God*, in Genesis 22 when Isaac is saved from sacrifice. In the New Testament, an angel announces Jesus' birth (Luke 2:10–11).

▼ANGEL PROTECTION
In this seventeenth-century image by Robert Fludd, the four archangels draw swords against the demonic powers that bring illness. Above them is the spirit of YHVH who listens to the prayers of humanity.

ANGELS LOCATED ON THE TREE OF LI[FE]

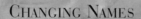

- CREATOR
- METATRON
- TZAPHKIEL
- HOLY SPIRITS OF THE FACE
- RAZIEL
- SAMAEL (EVIL)
- TZADKIEL (GOOD)
- MICHAEL
- RAFAEL (HEALING)
- ANGELS OF PRAISE
- URIEL (GRACE)
- GAVRIEL
- SERAPHIM
- HASHMALIM
- SANDALPHON
- BENEI ELOHIM
- TARSHISHIM
- ISHIM
- CHERUBIM

◄BLAKE'S ANGELS
This image by William Blake shows the Divine angels floating in water and the hellish angels enclosed in a fire of anger.

SPIRITUAL PARALLELS

In the Koran there are eight angels, instead of four, that support the Throne of Allah. These include Gavriel (Jibril) as chief, Michael, Israfil, and Azrael.

THE ARCHANGELS

METATRON guards the Throne of Glory and stands between Atzilut (Nearness) and Beriah (Creation). Metatron's tasks include recording good deeds and serving the Divine merkavah (chariot): it is thought that after Enoch's flesh was transformed into torches, he became Metatron.

MICHAEL (who is like God) stands at the right and presides over the people Israel and Tiferet. Michael is also the teacher of humanity and is said to have taught Adam how to till the soil.

RAFAEL (the healing of God) stands behind and presides over the spirits of humanity and Hod (Reverberation). Rafael is said to bring the prayers of humanity before God.

URIEL (the light of God) stands before the Throne and presides over the lights of the world, and Sheol (Underworld). Sometimes Uriel is called Haniel or Penuel (turning to God), who is set over repentance, grace, and the hope of eternal life and Netzach.

GAVRIEL (the strength of God) oversees paradise and the lower angels. Presiding over Yesod (Foundation), Gavriel also intercedes for humanity.

EXTRAS IN THE ANGELIC CAST

✡ Tzaphkiel (beholder of God), angel of Binah.

✡ Raziel (herald of God), angel of Chokhmah and responsible for secret wisdom.

✡ Samael, the fallen angel. Known as God's poisoner. Presides over Gevurah.

✡ Tzadkiel (righteousness of God) and angel of Chesed.

✡ Sandalphon, the angel of Malkhut, controls angels in the human world.

✡ Raguel, who takes revenge on the world of lights.

✡ Sariel, whose duties are not defined.

✡ Jeremiel, the angel who guards the souls of the underworld.

✡ The erelim, serafim, chayyot, ophanim, hamashalim, elim, and elohim, all of whom are the heavenly beings or malakhim.

✡ The benei erelim, the sons of the heavenly beings.

✡ The ishim, who are the manlike beings.

▲TZAPHKIEL
Tzaphkiel is the beholder of God and associated with Binah. This angel is an ideal subject of meditative thought and is associated with the qualities of understanding and intelligence.

INVOKING ANGELS THROUGH KABBALAH

Whereas the Talmud saw angels as God's instruments, medieval Kabbalists began to view them as instruments of man. Despite the prohibition against conjuring, Kabbalists in medieval Germany invoked the names of angels to make them visible and to enjoin them to act as agents.

Jewish law expressly forbids the practice of magic, with the Talmud promising benefits to those who abstain from such activities:

Everyone who does not practice magic enters a department of heaven to which even the ministering angels are not allowed access.

TALMUD NEDARIM 32a

Angelic names were viewed as the most sacred mystical element. The Book of Raziel begins with directions for invoking angels according to the day, month, and hour. Eliezer of Worms wrote in the *Book of Angels* that the whole world was full

of angels and demons, with guardian angels protecting every place and person. Each person was said to have his "angel of destiny," who brought about all the good and evil of his life.

As Kabbalah became more widespread throughout central and eastern Europe, so too obsession with angels seemed to dominate daily life. Amulets and charms were made with particular guardian angels in mind. Even today in ultra-Orthodox communities you can see amulets worn and displayed for protection.

THE HEAVENLY COURT

Besides offering praise to God and protecting righteous people, angels are also part of the heavenly system of justice. They sit in council when human beings are judged, to decide on the person's guilt or innocence. If 999 angels vote for conviction and only one votes for acquittal, God decides in favor of the human defendant. Similarly, angels can argue with God on behalf of a person. Further, they can appear as opposing counsel to evil angels who wish to prosecute in the Divine court.

FALLEN ANGELS AND EVIL

The story of fallen angels is first found in the Book of Enoch. Some 200 of the sons of heaven, among the guardian angels, lusted after human women and came down to earth to indulge with them. From these unions was born a generation of giants. A remnant of this intriguing story remains

▲ LIGHT OF GOD
Haniel, sometimes called Uriel, the light of God, is also associated with grace. In this Christian image, the angel hovers above the Throne, offering Divine grace and the hope of eternal life.

RECOGNIZING EVIL

Look honestly at what may sometimes motivate you and answer these questions:

✿ *Have you ever been tempted by the thought of a magic way to solve your dilemmas?*

✿ *Think about times you may have misused your will. How might you be guided by the presence of angels?*

✿ *If you can accept evil as part of yourself and the world, what can you do to minimize its power in your life?*

in Genesis 6:1–4, where the "Nefilim," or fallen ones, are described as heroes and men of renown.

In the apocalyptic literature, each of the fallen angels taught humanity a particular kind of evil, as well as the use of weapons. By the Middle Ages, several different stories had arisen to explain the Fall and the presence of evil. Satan, originally called Lucifer and one of God's closest angels, refused to submit to Adam and rebelled in pride. He was deposed and became the spirit of evil.

Kabbalah recognizes the pervasive power of evil, but sees it as something arising from within God, because it was a part of the Divine Creation. Evil can be opposed and counterbalanced by the force of Chesed (Mercy), the force of darkness by the torch of heavenly light.

◄ ANGELIC HEALING
Rafael is said to carry the energy of healing. Although not in direct contact with humanity, Rafael carries people's prayers to God, thus healing the spirit. You may wish to imagine and focus this healing power in your life as you contemplate the angelic image.

SPIRITUAL PARALLELS

The ancient Persian spirits of good, or benign immortals—Vohu-Mano (Good), Asha-Vahishta (Supreme Righteousness), Khshathra-Vairya (Ideal Dominion), Spenta-Aramaiti (Benign Piety), Haurvatat (Perfection), and Ameretat (Immortality)—can be compared to the biblical archangels.

The fetishes of African religions take the place of angels, although the supreme God is often surrounded by the souls of their ancestors.

Spirits similar to those in Kabbalah appear in Matthew 28:2–7 and Acts 12:15.

◄ PERSIAN TRADITION
This Persian image of the angelic world shows parallels to the story of Ezekiel's chariot. Flames surround the horse-god, ministering angels offer gifts, and archangels surround the throne.

THE ANGELS *in* YOUR LIFE

The Talmud (Niddah 30b) records that before people are born, being of pure spirit, they know everything; however, at the moment of birth, as they see the light of day, an angel strikes them above the lip and they forget everything. The whole of life is therefore spent trying to remember what we once knew.

Angels are not a theoretical construct in Kabbalah. They are a real and present part of earthly life. You may encounter an angel at any time, in the guise of a human or in some other form. What can you do to prepare yourself for such a meeting?

Jewish tradition includes a bedtime prayer that accompanies the nightly recitation of the statement of Jewish belief, the Shema. After blessing the Divine Spirit and commending oneself to God's care during sleep, the following is said to invoke the strength of the angels:

May Michael, the protector of God, be at my right hand; and Gavriel, the power of God, be at my left; before me, Uriel, the light of God; and behind me, Rafael, the healing of God. And above my head, may there be the indwelling presence of God, Shekhinat El.

FORMS OF PRAYER

▶ ANGEL BY
　YOUR SIDE

Sometimes angels appear at the darkest times of a person's life and it is easy to reject the help they offer. However, an angel can help you to transform your life, if you allow it to. Consider the consequences of letting angels into your life. Try to imagine that you have a guardian angel. What might he or she be like? Where in your life might you ask for angelic help? This modern angelic image is taken from the hit movie, City of Angels, *starring Nicholas Cage.*

▶ NEW MEANING

In this Christianized image of Jacob's dream, the fountain of the Church is placed at the confluence of the rivers. Angels moving up and down the ladder carry different aspects of Divine energy, visualized as fire and cloud at the top of the ladder. Apples and pomegranates recall both the Eden of the past and the splendor of Hod.

PREPARE TO MEET AN ANGEL

Think of the angelic qualities that surround you: strength, protection, light, grace, and healing. Along with these are the angelic energies of contemplation, good, and evil. Each morning, as you prepare to greet the world, you can also prepare yourself to encounter an angel. Give thanks for your safe return from sleep and acknowledge the angels that protect you.

You never know what an angel will look like, so prepare by opening yourself to the possibility of angelic help. You may wish to visualize angelic beings or repeat a phrase that reminds you of their presence and benevolent intentions. Walk through your day imagining the possibility that a stranger might be an angel sent to help you. Don't judge people so quickly and listen to strangers with a new ear of possibility. Ask yourself what it is possible to learn from new encounters.

CHAPTER FIVE

MODELS AND MEANINGS

Kabbalah has always attracted seekers and scholars of many different approaches. Over the centuries, the search for knowledge has crossed intellectual and cultural boundaries. Early Jewish mysticism shows clear parallels with second-century Greek Gnosticism and earlier Persian religious traditions.

Sects created their own models to describe their theology and practice, some of which are examined in this chapter. We will look at some Jewish models of mystical understanding and then explore connections with the wisdom of other spiritual traditions.

▶ STUDY THE STARS
Astrology and astronomy have always played a key part in spiritual traditions. Kabbalah is no exception and bases many of its theories on astrological notions. This fourteenth-century Spanish illustration shows the vital study of the stars, with the teacher guiding his students through their lessons, both academically and spiritually.

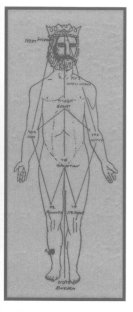

▲ HUMAN ESSENCE
*Primordial Man is seen
here as a representation
of Divine Will. The
sefirot are superimposed
over the body in a way
that makes the Tree of
Life relate to our own
physical form.*

CROSS-CULTURAL MYSTICISM

*Since written history began, humanity has tried to understand
the relationship between the vastness of the cosmos, creation, and
life on Earth. Many traditions have embraced mysticism as a way
of answering the cosmic questions. Kabbalah is one path to truth.
The Tree of Life, the central Kabbalistic image, can be found in
varied forms in cultures worldwide.*

THE MYSTERY OF THE CHARIOT

Kabbalah arose and developed within Jewish tradition, with the teachings of the Torah, the later prophetic writings of the Bible and Apocrypha, and the three works—*Sefer Yetzirah*, *Sefer ha-Bahir*, and the *Zohar*—as its central core. Thus the Kabbalistic models are uniquely Jewish. However, no wisdom exists in a vacuum. In each century, cultures have met and exotic ideas have mingled with familiar mind-sets.

For the early Jewish mystics of the first and second centuries C.E., esoteric apocalyptic literature was the source of mystical knowledge and practice. The Book of Enoch and the vision of the Chariot (Merkavah) stimulated the development of Merkavah mysticism.

UPPER AND LOWER WORLDS

The concept of movement from lower to upper worlds became a central goal for the mystics, who created meditations and other rituals to facilitate their own spiritual ascent. A variety of scriptural narratives fueled these practices:

Enoch had a vision of an enthroned "son of man." When Enoch died, he was transfigured and ascended to the place of the Throne, where some say he became Metatron, the scribe to God.

Elijah the prophet, who lived in the ninth century B.C.E., was said to have drawn down the fire of God to kindle his sacrifice and thus defeat the 450 prophets of Baal. As his reward, he was drawn up to heaven on a whirlwind in a chariot of fire drawn by horses of fire. The fiery chariot is the vehicle for transfiguration. It is also an emanation of Divine light.

Ezekiel, who prophesied during the Babylonian exile some 300 years later, beheld a vision of the Chariot (Merkavah) made of four levels: the wheels, the living creatures, the firmament, and the Divine Throne. The mysteries of the Throne and the path of ascent toward union with the Divine light became the central concern of Merkavah mysticism.

The Merkavah mystics tried to connect with the all-powerful transcendent God of the upper world. The Hekhalot (halls) literature established a world extending through the seven palaces in the uppermost of the seven firmaments. Hosts of angels populated the palaces, and rivers of fire flowed down from the Chariot. It was up through this

◄ EZEKIEL'S VISION
Prior to Kabbalah,
Jewish mysticism was
known as The Work of
the Chariot. The title
was inspired by the
vision of Ezekiel whose
story was the focus of
the early mystics. In this
seventeenth-century
image from the Beur
Bible, the four elements
represent the four worlds.

world to the Throne that the mystics tried to ascend, to experience the "One Who Sits on the Throne." From this vision arose the expression "to be in seventh heaven," meaning a place of ecstasy.

GNOSTICISM

Gnosticism, a Christian sect of the second century C.E., had many points of contact with early Jewish mysticism. Gnosticism held that the key to liberation of the soul could only be through knowledge. Gnostics developed the concept that the soul, or divine seed of God, was imprisoned in the body, or evil matter. Agape, mystical love, was the route to knowledge of God and the way to release the soul

from the confines of evil matter.

Note the parallels with the Kabbalistic notion of the good and evil inclinations—*yetzer ha'tov* and *yetzer ha'ra*. At the very beginnings of Christianity, these ideas moved between the different sects, and mystical practices embraced the teachings of many varied traditions.

SPIRITUAL PARALLELS

The Rosicrucians of the seventeenth century believed in upward progress through twelve dimensions or degrees of mastery to achieve cosmic consciousness. Perfection was attained through reincarnation.

THE RISE *of* SACRED NUMEROLOGY

In the first few centuries C.E., *Jewish theology flourished. The appearance of the* Sefer Yetzirah *stimulated a whole new approach to mysticism. The concept of the sefirot and the thirty-two paths to wisdom based on the Hebrew alphabet led to great creativity with both letters and numbers.*

▶ THE ABACUS
Dating from ancient times, the abacus became the traditional counting tool of the Middle East and the Orient. It undoubtedly played a role in the practice of numerology where addition was a primary ritual in the calculation of sacred numbers.

▼ WHEEL OF LETTERS
This diagram shows the Hebrew letters arranged in a circular pattern as an aid to spiritual contemplation. It is taken from a 1592 Polish edition of the key Kabbalistic work Orchard of Pomegranates *by Moses Cordovero.*

THE EMERGENCE OF GEMATRIA

Mystical practices were designed to experience the power of the paths. These were based on the manipulation of the letters that were chanted and repeated. Mystics of the seventh to eleventh centuries created a range of apocalyptic literature. Rich angelology and demonology developed, and magical incantations became more popular, as the previously secret notions of the supernal world came into popular consciousness.

One new trend that emerged between the eighth and eleventh centuries C.E. greatly influenced Kabbalah. This was the rise of gematria, an attempt to elucidate, through numbers, connections between the Divine names and verses in the Bible. Sacred numerology was not a form of divination, in that its purpose was never to tell the future. Rather, the Kabbalists, especially the thirteenth-century German school under Eliezer of Worms, tried to unlock hidden Biblical meanings.

UNLOCKING THE SECRETS

The letters of the Hebrew alphabet were assigned numerical values in accordance with their order. In addition, each letter had a pictorial representation with profound significance. For example, *alef*, the first letter, equals 1 and represents an ox and expansive, thrusting energy. *Bet (vet)*, the second letter, equals 2 and represents a house and passive qualities.

Although different Kabbalists established their own systems for using the letters and their numeric values, the intention remained steady—to uncover the secret meaning encoded in the Bible.

ABULAFIA: KABBALISTIC MASTER

Abraham Abulafia was born in Spain in 1240—which corresponds to the year 5000 in the Hebrew calendar—and the new millennium was seen as auspicious and portentous. He saw himself as an enlightened prophet and gained both adherents and severe critics during and after his lifetime.

Abulafia's approach to meditation was through the permutation of letters of Divine names, incorporating bodily movements, similar to Yoga. His practices are clearly described in his work *Life of the Future World*. The method uses seventy-two

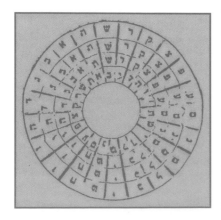

FINDING SIGNIFICANCE *in* NUMEROLOGY

These questions can help your perceptions to expand:

✡ *Are there any numbers that seem to recur in your life?*

✡ *Can you allow yourself time to look for connections between seemingly unrelated things in your life?*

THE 22 HEBREW LETTERS AND THEIR MEANING

Hebrew letter	name	numerical value	pronunciation	significance	classification
א	alef	1	soft breathed a	ox	mother
ב, ב	bet (vet)	2	b (v)	house	double
ג	gimel	3	g	camel	double
ד	dalet	4	d	door	double
ה	hay	5	h	window	elemental
ו	vav	6	v	hook	elemental
ז	zayin	7	z	weapon	elemental
ח	chet	8	ch as in loch	fence	elemental
ט	tet	9	t	serpent	elemental
י	yod	10	y	hand	elemental
כ, ך	khaf, final khaf	20	kh	palm	double
ל	lamed	30	l	ox-goad	elemental
מ, ם	mem, final mem	40	m	water	mother
נ, ן	nun, final nun	50	n	fish	elemental
ס	samech	60	s	prop	elemental
ע	ayin	70	silent or a	eye	elemental
פ, פ, ף	pay (fay, final fay)	80	p (f, f)	mouth	double
צ, ץ	tzadi, final tzadi	90	tz	fishhook	elemental
ק	koof	100	k	back of head	elemental
ר	resh	200	r	head	double
ש, שׂ	shin (sin)	300	sh (s)	tooth	mother
ת	tav	400	t	cross	double

combinations of the Divine name, based on three verses from Exodus. According to Abulafia, the name is to be written and chanted as follows:

Prepare yourself, unify your heart, and purify your body. Choose a special place for yourself, where your voice will not be heard by anyone else. Meditate alone, with no one else present … Do not reveal your secret to anyone … As a result of these permutations, your heart will become extremely warm. From the permutations you will gain new knowledge that you never learned from human traditions nor derived from intellectual analysis. When you experience this, you are prepared to receive the influx.

MEDITATION AND KABBALAH

KAPLAN

SPIRITUAL PARALLELS

Pythagoras, the originator of numerology in Greece, believed that the whole universe could be expressed in numbers. The number 888 equals the name of Jesus in Greek and represented the higher mind, while 666 represented the mortal mind. For the Greeks, 10 was a perfect number, paralleling the perfection of the ten sefirot.

Sacred numerology includes a fascination with sacred geometry. The Egyptian pyramids and tombs are physical representations of numerical relationships that were believed to be sacred.

THE MYSTICAL POWER *of* NUMBERS

Jewish tradition prohibits the use of magic, divination, or the occult for the purpose of knowing the future. Nevertheless, many Kabbalistic practices arose in response to the natural desire for reassurance and protection, using amulets with mystical designs and letters, and incantations to protect and guide.

THE POWER OF TEN

It is easy to see how the Ten Commandments became associated with the ten sefirot. Ten is a perfect number, because when the two digits are added, 1 + 0, the result is 1, representing the one God. The *Sefer Yetzirah* establishes the importance of the number 10 in the first chapter:

Ten sefirot of Nothingness

in the number of ten fingers: five opposite five

with a singular covenant precisely in the middle

in the circumcision of the tongue and

in the circumcision of the sexual organ.

SEFER YETZIRAH 1:3

It is possible to meditate on the ten fingers, the ten toes, the tongue, and the penis. These add up to 22, parallel to the twenty-two letters of the Hebrew alphabet and the twenty-two paths. Additionally, the ten toes represent the ten sefirot and can be the focus of a meditation that concentrates spiritual energy into the sexual organ.

▼ GREEK NUMBERS
The Pythagorean "Chi" (X) is a parallel form of sacred geometry, as it represents the cosmic soul. From the central point of zero, all of creation unfolds, seen here as relationships between fractions and multiples. The form ascends from one as perfect squares.

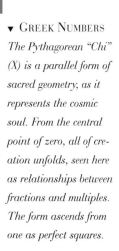

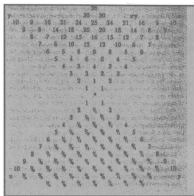

THE DIVINE NAME YHVH

Consider the numeric value of the Hebrew word for the Divine name of YHVH:
the letter *yod* has the power of ten
the letter *hay* has the power of five
the letter *vav* has the power of six
the letter *hay* has the power of five.
Therefore, the total value of YHVH is 26. Using the approach of sacred geometry, 26 is taken as the sacred mean between 13 and 52. The number 13 connects to the thirteen lunar months and 52 to the solar weeks in a year. Thus YHVH is at the center of the year and the essence of the Sun and Moon, which light up our world. YHVH is the essential source of that and all light.

THE POWER OF LOVE

Two important words are linked to the Divine name of the Tetragrammaton through the wonders of gematria. These are the word *love*, which in Hebrew is *ahavah*, and has a value of 13, and the word *one*, or *echad*, that also has a value of 13. Thus *love* and *one* are equal and together add up to 26, the numeric equivalent of YHVH. From this is deduced that God is One and God is Love. Love

ABULAFIA'S GEMATRIA

These examples will give you some idea of the depth of Abulafia's gematria. It is dependent on a pure heart and knowledge of Scripture, as otherwise there is a danger that it can be used to manipulate and distort.

✡ *The Hebrew letters for the word* Shaddai, *meaning God of Might, equal 314. This is the same value as the Hebrew word for Metatron, angel of the Throne.*

✡ *Gavriel is the archangel who teaches God's mystery. His name in Hebrew equals 246 and is linked to the verse in Numbers 12:6, "I will make Myself known to him in a vision … " The Hebrew word for vision is* mareh *and also equals 246.*

✡ *Taken from the Sefer Yetzirah, Abulafia gave numeric meaning to each phrase of the following quotation:*

"the mystery of the twelve breaths,	*= 818*
the 72 Divine names,	*= 818*
the mystery of all the letters	*= 828*
depends on twenty-two breaths	*= 828*
which are under the glory."	*= 828*

becomes one of the routes to *yichud*—unity with the four worlds and God. This can be seen by adding together the digits of 13, thus 1 + 3 = 4.

TRUTH

Another powerful example of gematria is contained within the words *coal*, or *gachelet*, which has a value of 441, and *truth*, or *emet*, which also has a value of 441. The interpretation of this correspondence is that *truth* is said to burn like a flaming *coal* and bind all opposites together. In addition, *emet* consists of the first, last, and middle letters of the Hebrew alphabet, thus encompassing the beginning and end of all things.

The word *emet* became a focus for the Kabbalists of Eastern Europe, who manipulated the letters to create the Golem, a legendary being capable of enacting the will of its creator. On its brow was engraved *emet*, and it was only destroyed by removing the *alef*, thus taking away the creative breath, to leave *met*, meaning death.

TORAH

The Torah contains 613 commandments, of which 365 are negative prohibitions and 248 are positive prescriptions. These are said to correspond to the

▲ TEN DIGITS
The power of ten is manifested in our ten fingers and ten toes. Take time to contemplate your own fingers when studying the power of the ten sefirot.

days of the year and the number of bones in the body (although that number is actually 206). The gematria of the word *Torah* is 611, almost equivalent to the number of commandments. One conclusion from this is that living life according to the Torah leads to the essence of Divine teaching.

SPIRITUAL PARALLELS

In Christianity, the dove is the symbol of the Holy Spirit. The letters of the Greek word for dove, peristera, add up to 801, as do the first and last letters of the Greek alphabet, alpha and omega. In the Book of Revelation, Jesus Christ says, "I am the Alpha and the Omega" (Revelation 1:8, 21:6, 22:13).

Far Eastern sacred geometric designs of mandalas and yantras feature the hexagram, also a part of Kabbalistic structures. Hexagrams do not appear in Egyptian or Greek sacred geometry.

KABBALAH *and the* CHARKA SYSTEM

▶ PARALLEL POINTS
The chakras and the Tree of Life are two divergent systems whose structures show striking parallels. Both recognize the existence of centers of energy which have a significant impact on physical, emotional, and spiritual health.

In most spiritual traditions, models of reality develop in conjunction with a belief system. These models often represent the human world, as well as the metaphysical universe. They are used as a guide to contemplation. Kabbalists came to view the Tree of Life as a model of the universe that also truthfully represents the life and structure of human beings.

PHYSICAL AND METAPHYSICAL

The Tree of Life has a psychobiological application, which maps the human body in relation to physical, emotional, and spiritual health and well-being. The vibrational energies that interact in the worlds of Yetzirah (Formation) and Assiyah (Action) can also be represented in terms of the structure and processes of the mind, emotions, and body.

In the Hindu and Buddhist traditions of the Far East, the chakra system is the model for understanding how *ch'i*, the life force, flows throughout the human body and the universe. *Chakra* comes from the Sanskrit word for wheel and is visualized as a whirling vortex, spoked wheel, or open lotus flower that receives, distributes, and transforms energy. There are seven

major chakras and hundreds of minor ones, existing in and influencing the realm of the etheric, astral, and mental bodies as well as the physical.

The chakra concept corresponds to the Kabbalistic view of the four worlds, with the Tree of Life manifest and active in each of them. Just as the sefirot form a vertical pattern, so the chakras lie vertically along the spine, from the base to the crown, and are connected to each other and the rest of the body by channels of subtle energy.

Like the sefirot of the Tree of Life, the chakra system is invisible to the human eye, although some highly sensitive people claim to be able to see or feel the energy that emanates from the chakras. The system underlies the complementary medical practices of acupuncture, reflexology, shiatsu, and some forms of healing and meditation.

CHAKRA POSITION AND ASSOCIATIONS	CORRESPONDING SEFIROT
CROWN *Above the head* *Enlightenment and cosmic consciousness* *Purple or white*	**CROWN/KETER** *Top of head* *God's will* *White/black*
BROW OR THIRD EYE *Between the eyes* *Intelligence, intuition, and psychic powers* *Yellow-rose and blue-purple* *Pituitary and pineal glands*	**CHOKHMAH AND BINAH** *Right and left ears* *Wisdom and understanding* *Blue and green* *Consciousness and feeling*
THROAT *Throat* *Creativity, expression, search for truth* *Silvery blue* *Thyroid and parathyroid glands*	**DA'AT (NON-SEFIRAH)** *n/a* *Knowledge emerging from God* *n/a* *Ego, thought, action*
N/A *n/a* *n/a* *n/a* *n/a*	**GEVURAH AND CHESED** *Left and right shoulders* *Strength and mercy, creation* *Red and white* *Metabolic processes*
HEART *Heart* *Higher consciousness, unconditional love, immunity to disease* *Green and golden* *Thymus gland and immunity system*	**TIFERET** *Heart* *Beauty and self-consciousness in the heart* *White* *Central nervous system*
SOLAR PLEXUS *Above the navel* *Emotions and sense of identity* *Yellow, green, light red* *Adrenal system, pancreas, liver, and stomach*	**HOD AND NETZACH** *Left and right legs* *Flexibility, determination* *Green and red* *Cells and organs*
SACRAL-HARA *Above the genitals* *Sexuality and reproduction* *Orangey red* *Overall health, liver, pancreas, spleen, digestion*	**YESOD** *Above the genitals* *Perception of the world* *White* *Autonomic nervous system, spiritual aspiration*
ROOT *Base of spine, below genitals* *Survival instincts, animal nature, taste, and smell* *Reddish orange* *Self-preservation*	**MALKHUT** *Between the feet* *Perception* *White* *Skeleton, skin, sense organs*

THE ENNEAGRAM

The enneagram is a geometric model of the universe. It was brought to the West early in the twentieth century by Georgei Gurdjieff, a Russian mystic who emigrated to France in 1922. Although an earlier form of enneagram was created in 1665 by the Jesuit Athanasius Kircher, its source lies in Islamic Sufi mysticism.

SUFISM AND THE ENNEAGRAM

The roots of the enneagram system lie in Sufism, a mystical branch of Islam that arose in the ninth century C.E. as a reaction against formal Muslim theology. The term comes from *suf*, the Arabic word for wool, and symbolized the simple wool garments worn by the Sufis. The Sufis embrace asceticism and mystical love as the path to oneness with Allah. The path to Divine knowledge is through reading, study, prayer, and *dhikr*, the constant repetition of God's name and passages from the Koran. The Sufi path is a lifetime's occupation, as it helps the individual to remember that people are one with God. The parallels with the Kabbalistic path of contemplation, devotion, and action are striking.

LOOKING AT THE ENNEAGRAM

The word *enneagram* comes from Greek and means "nine points." It represents both the cosmos and the human psyche and combines two ancient laws, which may derive from the sacred geometry of Pythagoras (sixth century B.C.E.).

The Law of the Triad states that three forces regulate everything that happens in the world:
the active, initiating force;
the receptive, processing force;
the reconciling, balancing force.

This can be represented in philosophical terms by thesis, antithesis, and synthesis. In order for change and development to occur, the two opposing forces must be reconciled by a third, which allows both new understanding and new energy for a new reality. People can rise from their lower carnal bodies through their emotional bodies and on to their spiritual bodies by working on themselves, a form of alchemical transmutation.

The Law of the Octave expresses the truth of musical reality. A vibrating string, divided into eight sections by seven frets along it, will increase in pitch from one section to the next in a precise mathematical ratio. The simple unity of the vibration of the single string becomes a complex, densely packed series of harmonics.

According to Gurdjieff, each point of the enneagram is connected to the others in a sequence based on the recurring decimal created by dividing 1 by 7. The fraction $\frac{1}{7} = 0.1428571428571$. Thus the sequence of points is 1, 4, 2, 8, 5, 7. Points 3 and 6, he said, were the points of infusion of new energy required to keep the system functioning. Gurdjieff taught that people cross the intervals of development by means of shocks given by "a Man who Knows." These shocks are the new energy that allows change to occur. Gurdjieff called his system the Fourth Way, the Way of the Cunning Man, to distinguish it from the three traditional paths to spiritual enlightenment, the paths of the fakir, the monk, and the yogi. He considered his way superior because people do not need to undergo physical, emotional, or intellectual suffering in order to harmonize their paths.

◄ DERVISH DANCE
Sufi monks, or dervishes,
practice ecstatic dancing
to attain higher levels of
spiritual consciousness.

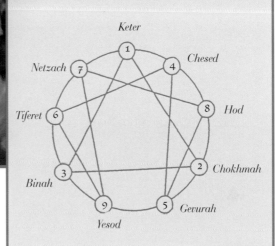

LINKS WITH THE TREE OF LIFE

Both the enneagram and the Tree of Life have One
as their Divine Source—in the enneagram, the
Essential One, from which the many personality
characteristics resonate; in Kabbalah, the One
God from whom emanate the Divine attributes of
the sefirot. Just as the ten sefirot represent ten
Divine qualities or attributes (see Chapter Two),
so the enneagram has been interpreted to represent nine pairs of qualities manifest in the world.

Both the sefirotic Tree of Life and the enneagram are based on systems in which there is
dynamic internal interaction. The three souls of
Kabbalah—*nefesh* (soul of the living being), *ruach*
(middle soul), and *neshama* (higher soul)—parallel the three centers of intelligence of the enneagram—the belly (physical survival), the heart
(emotional core), and the head (mental center).

SHATTERING AND REPAIR

Kabbalah identifies the shattering of the vessels
as the cause of the scattering of Divine sparks
throughout the world. The task of Kabbalah is
to repair the world (tikkun olam) through the
reunification of all the scattered sparks (yichud).
In the enneagram system, the individual loses
the concept of Essence, or Oneness, during child-
hood and becomes fixated on particular patterns
that shatter the individual's spiritual wholeness.
The enneagram path to reunification consists of

recognizing our limiting patterns and moving from
our fixations and passions toward our corresponding virtues, thus enabling us to reconnect with the
Holy Essence and find Oneness.

▲ ENNEAGRAM LINKS
The above arrangement
shows Gurdjieff's place-
ment of the sefirot on the
enneagram. The tenth
sefirah of Malkhut is the
actual circle joining the
points together.

MOVING BEYOND LIMITATIONS

Explore your capacity for change by asking
yourself these questions:

✡ *Looking at the enneagram diagrams, which points*
best represent your fixations and your passions?

✡ *What can you do to release yourself from these limita-*
tions and move toward the corresponding virtues?

✡ *What are some of the shocks you have experienced*
recently that have helped to move you on?

THE ART *of* ALCHEMY

Alchemy is the art of transmuting base metals into gold. Its name comes from the Arabic al-kimiya (the art of transmutation), and the Greek khemia (the melting and alloying of metals). While alchemy was the precursor of chemistry, it also had a spiritual dimension. The roots of alchemy lie in many traditions: Hermetics, Gnosticism, Islam, Taoism, Yoga, and Kabbalah.

▲ SEVEN PHASES
This seventeenth-century alchemic illustration shows the seven phases of the alchemist's work. Starting from lower left, the old man, Saturn, is shown at the beginning of inner development, the phase of putrefaction. Moving clockwise, the doves can be seen lifting the crown. The process ends with rebirth, shown as the young man.

ALCHEMY IN EUROPE

It is likely that alchemy began in the fertile relationship between Greek and Egyptian theology from about 200 B.C.E. through the early centuries of the Common Era. From Egypt came the fundamental principle that a Divine force created the world from "first matter," a chaotic mass. The process of *solva et coagula* (dissolving and combining) can reduce all things to first matter or transmute them to higher substances.

By the twelfth century alchemy had spread throughout Europe and become a respectable science. Its peak was from the fourteenth to the seventeenth centuries, when it often combined with the Christian and occult practices of Kabbalah and thereby attracted the strong disapproval of the Catholic Church.

The principles of alchemy were expounded by Nicholas Flamel in the fourteenth century, who was believed to have achieved the transmutation of mercury into silver and gold. The means of this remarkable transformation was through the use of the philosophers' stone, a legendary catalyst, substance, or chemical preparation. In the seven-teenth century, John Frederick Helvetius, a physician to the Prince of Orange, claimed that he had been given a piece of the philosophers' stone and had succeeded in creating gold from lead.

Besides trying to create gold, the alchemists sought to create the elixir of life, a potion for immortality made by dissolving some of the philosophers' stone in wine. This elixir was said by the great Swiss physician Paracelsus to "cleanse the whole body of impurities by the introduction of new and more youthful forces which it joins to the nature of man."

THE PRINCIPLES OF ALCHEMY

Underlying the process of alchemical transmutation was the concept that everything is composed of three substances: sulphur, representing the soul and the fiery male principle; mercury, representing spirit and the watery female principle; and salt, representing the body. Separating these substances from compounds and recombining them according to astrological signs and sacred instructions enabled the alchemist to enter the mysteries of the spiritual world.

ALCHEMY IN INDIA AND CHINA

Indian alchemy goes back to the beginnings of Ayurvedic medicine before 1000 B.C.E. It was a union of male and female principles (Shiva and Parvati) resulting in enlightenment. Through the

◄ PHILOSOPHICAL TREE
The seventeenth-century alchemic work The Anatomy of Gold, *shows the sefirotic Tree as the basis for alchemical transformation. The dissolving and binding powers sit on opposite branches, with Mercury across from Sulphur, and solid sulphur, son of the sun, triumphant at the top with the crowns of the animal, vegetable, and mineral kingdoms.*

practice of Tantric Yoga, it was believed possible to achieve immortality.

The classic Chinese text on alchemy, *Nei P'ien*, was written in 320 C.E. by Ko Hung. In it the alchemist sought to develop supernormal powers that enabled him to achieve a state of timelessness to be spent with the Immortals. The processes of alchemy created, in physical form, elixirs that paralleled the intangible life force, *ch'i*.

ALCHEMY AND KABBALAH

The earliest recorded alchemist was Maria Hebraea (Maria the Hebrew) in Hellenistic Egypt around 300 C.E. Her teachings show clear links to ideas that later become part of Kabbalistic doctrine. There is a clear relationship between the Hebrew word for heavens, *shamayim*, and the words for fire, *aish*, and water, *mayim*. The coming together and balancing of opposing elements or forces clearly parallels the balance between the two pillars of the sefirotic Tree and the ascending and descending movement of the angels and Kabbalists. In both alchemy and Kabbalah, the goal is unification and transformation.

SPIRITUAL PARALLELS

Alchemy postulates that all things are composed of three elements: sulphur = soul = fiery male principle; mercury = spirit = watery female principle; and salt = body = solid earth. These are separated and recombined to create transmutation.

ALTERING *the* ESSENCE

Think about the possibility of allowing your untapped potential to blossom:

✡ *Using the metaphor of the philosophers' stone, what might be a catalyst for you to transform yourself to achieve your higher potential?*

✡ *What aspects of your life represent fire, water, earth, and air?*

✡ *How do they combine and what is the result?*

ZEN

Zen is a form of Buddhism that has developed into different schools. The term comes from the Chinese ch'an *and the Sanskrit* dhyana, *meaning meditation and the consciousness that results from meditation in order to realize the "Buddha nature." The aim of Zen is the attainment of consciousness with no self. Kabbalah aims at consciousness with the merging of self with the Divine.*

PRINCIPLES OF ZEN

Zen is not a religion and has no scripture as authority, but is rather a daily spiritual practice which frees the individual from the delusion of truth as citadel and icon. Two of the main schools of Zen are Rinzai and Soto Zen. Rinzai originated in the experience of Rinzai, who when he asked his master to teach him the essential truth of Buddha nature, was beaten soundly. Ultimately, the shock of this direct experience enabled Rinzai to achieve enlightenment. Today, at least in the West, Rinzai is gentler, but still works through direct experience.

Soto Zen originated in China, founded by Tsao Shan and Tung Shan. In Japan it was established by Dogen in 1227 as a sect of Zen. There are now more than 15,000 Soto Zen temples. Soto Zen mainly comprises the practice of *zazen*, or sitting meditation. The training consists of passing through five stages, each a higher level of understanding and consciousness. The metaphor for the process is the relationship between host and guest, or a prince and his minister. The host/prince represents our real being in spiritual reality. The guest/minister is the deluded, material, mental human being living in the world.

Stage 1: Discover there is such a thing as spiritual reality and a higher self greater than one's "little self down here." It is represented by the apparent over the real and a large area of darkness over a small amount of light. Darkness refers to the unseeing self and the paradox of the simultaneous absorption of everything and nothingness.

Stage 2: Recognition and acceptance that one is the guest/minister and welcomes the spiritual host/prince as one's teacher. Realizing that one is only a guest in the world, the practitioner aims to set aside personal desire in order to serve the host properly and respectfully. The higher and greater principle of light overwhelms the insignificant darkness that is the human being. As attachments die away, one "becomes like a withered log."

Stage 3: Spiritual reality becomes real in the world, so the withered log blossoms again, as the guest/minister realizes that this higher reality is within the individual and not somewhere beyond. The interests of the host become the interests of the guest, which are shown as a small dot of dark (not seeing) within a circle of light (enlightenment). The intellect ceases to be the motivating factor in life as the practitioner moves toward constant awareness.

◄ ZEN DIVINITY
*While there is no divinity
in Zen, the pagoda (far
left) represents levels of
reality that rise from the
human realm to the
perfection of nothingness,
a concept similar to the
Kabbalistic four worlds.*

*The Taming of the Bull
(left) is a series of
illustrations depicting the
Zen process of
enlightenment. In this,
the seventh of the series,
the herdsman is at peace
after meditation, and the
bull, symbolizing the
spirit, is tethered safely.*

Stage 4: At this point the guest and host become one: the self is effaced and merges with the spiritual reality. The individual no longer has any personal or separate desires. The black dot disappears, leaving a circle of all light.

Stage 5: With the realization of oneness with the host/prince comes the consciousness of oneness with all reality, both animate and inanimate. Wrong ceases to be a concept, as it is merely a distorted seeing, and light and dark merge. The symbol is a black circle, which includes everything.

The parallels with the Kabbalistic aim of yichud are quite obvious. Also the idea of light overcoming darkness has echoes of the ascent toward the light, which is part of Merkavah mysticism and Kabbalah.

Seeming paradox is an essential part of Soto Zen called koan. The koan is an exercise of the mind that goes beyond thought and logic, a form of meditation and contemplation whose answer cannot be reached through the exercise of the literal, logical mind. The Kabbalistic concepts of tzimtzum and the opposition and balance of the left and right sefirotic pillars of the Tree of Life also create apparent paradoxes for the Kabbalist to contemplate. The internal and external forms of meditation that form a part of Zen are both mirrored in the hitboddedut and hitbonnenut forms present in Kabbalah. Contemplation of texts, emptying the mind, focusing on light, and ascent are practiced in both traditions.

STAGES *of* UNDERSTANDING

Examine your spiritual experiences as you answer these questions:

✡ *What aspects of yourself do you think would fall away if you were able to practice the Zen form of consciousness?*

✡ *What are your delusions of belief and the apparent realities that you take as truths?*

✡ *When you meditate, what happens to you when you focus on a paradoxical question or statement?*

THE *I CHING* and YIN AND YANG

The I Ching, *or Book of Changes, is a Chinese philosophical system from the Taoist tradition dating back almost 5,000 years. Tao, meaning "the way," is the ultimate reality that is the origin of everything. The* I Ching *suggests that the universe—past, present, and future—is determined by the laws of change. Causality rather than coincidence is responsible for events.*

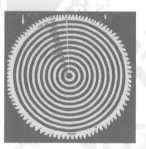

▲ CORRESPONDENCES
There are clear links between the I Ching *trigrams (above) and the Kabbalistic idea of Ayn Sof, or Divine will without end (below). At the center of the trigrams lies the yin/yang circle, symbolizing oneness, while the Ayn Sof is made up of concentric circles starting with the area of Malkhut and moving out to Ayn Sof.*

YIN AND YANG

The structure underlying the *I Ching* is the interrelationship of yin and yang. Yin is the earth principle, expressed as a white curved part of a circle. It represents passive, receptive female energy. Yang is the complement of yin. Expressed as the complementary black portion of the circle, it is the heaven principle, consisting of active, creative, or expansive male energy. The symbol of yin/yang demonstrates that within each there is a small dot of the other: i.e. within yin is the lesser yang, and within yang the lesser yin.

HOW THE *I CHING* IS USED

The *I Ching* is used as an oracle for divination and to chart the progress of a person's life. It consists of sixty-four hexagrams, each consisting of six solid or broken lines; these are patterns formed by throwing three coins three times or forty-nine sticks. There are four kinds of lines: broken lines representing yin; unbroken lines indicating yang; moving yin, which becomes yang; and moving yang, which becomes yin. The hexagram always moves from the bottom up, from earth to heaven. For each possible combination of lines or coins, the *I Ching* gives a name and a text summarizing what it means, along with advice pertaining to each hexagram. The individual asks a question before throwing the sticks and uses the generalized commentaries to stimulate the right side of the brain in order to

develop a personal interpretation for the specific question posed. It is the internal work done by the questioner that gives meaning to the data from the book. Only by going within can one find the true answers to questions of spiritual truth.

THE *I CHING* AND KABBALAH

Although the *I Ching* and Kabbalah are very different traditions, parallels can be seen between the structures underlying the two systems. Yin and yang are complementary principles, apparently in opposition. Similarly the Tree of Life includes the opposite yet complementary pillars of severity or restriction, which is female energy similar to yin, and of expansiveness, which is male energy like yang. Both traditions seek unification through balance with the ineffable truth. Ayn Sof and the Tao are both unnameable, indescribable, and beyond understanding.

MEDITATION AS THE PATH TO TRUTH

Both Kabbalah and Taoism prescribe meditation as an essential element of the work of spiritual purification. Both Taoist and Kabbalistic meditation include concentration, breath control, and purification of heart and mind. They differ, on the other hand, in that Taoist daily practice includes *wu wei*, or nonaction, a form of passivity that flows with the energy (*ch'i*) of the universe. Kabbalah, however, prescribes action that arises out of contemplation and devotion as part of the

▲ THE EXPERIENCE OF TAI CHI EXERCISE
Tai chi is a physical and spiritual discipline that benefits both motivation and concentration. In China, it is commonly practiced as a communal experience.

task of tikkun olam, the repair of the world. However, at times in its development, the practice of Kabbalah has also included asceticism and withdrawal from society and worldly life.

◄ YIN AND YANG
Both the visual symbol and the concept of yin and yang represent ultimate oneness and the merging of light and dark energies.

OPENING *to* OPPOSITES

Answer these questions as you consider the patterns that have repeated in your life:

✿ *Can you identify the ways in which masculine and feminine energy express themselves in your life?*

✿ *Are you generally more outward-reaching and aggressive, or more passive and receptive?*

✿ *How would your relationships change if you were to incorporate more of the less familiar energy in your thoughts and actions?*

✿ *Have you ever consciously practiced nonaction? How might it feel to flow with the energy of the universe?*

ASTROLOGY *and the* ZODIAC

Astrology as a system of divination dates back almost 5,000 years. The zodiac is a map of the stars based on a band of twelve constellations on the ecliptic. Astrology is based on the belief that the stars, planets, and other heavenly bodies influence earthly events. The position of, and relationship between, the celestial bodies can be mapped, from which readings can be made.

▲ PHYSICAL ZODIAC
Astrologers believed that the stellar constellations governed the workings of the body. In this French woodcut of 1499, the zodiac signs are placed on the human body and are linked in a similar way as the sefirot and Primordial Man.

JUDAISM AND ASTROLOGY

A story from the *Talmud* gives an indication of Jewish attitudes toward astrology:

Two Jewish woodcutters stopped at an inn on their way to the forest. A Chaldean offered to cast their horoscopes and having done so, foretold that they would die that very day. The Jews went to their work and on their way encountered an old man who was desperately hungry. They took out their loaf of bread that was to serve them for sustenance that day, cut it in half and gave one half to the old man. That evening they came again to the inn and found that the astrologer was still there. He looked at them in amazement as they dropped their loads of wood onto the ground, and was even more surprised when out of each load, as it broke open, fell half of a very poisonous, but undoubtedly dead, snake. "What have you done to avert the decree of your death?" he asked, so they recounted the events of the day. He exclaimed, "Blessed be the God of the Hebrews, who turns the stars from their courses for the sake of half a loaf of bread."

QUOTED IN BILL HEILBRONN,

GOD IS NOT AN UNCLE

From this story, it is clear that the practice of astrology was familiar, because the men allowed the Chaldean to cast their horoscopes. However, the outcome of the story indicates that Jewish belief and practice, here an act of loving-kindness and charity, were viewed as a superior way of ensuring one's future.

ASTROLOGY AND KABBALAH

Astrology was certainly a part of the belief and practices of the Kabbalists, despite the vehement condemnation of Maimonides. Rabbi Rava bar Joseph bar Chama (fourth century C.E.), some Babylonians believed a person's fortune depended not on merit but on the individual ruling planet. Both the *Sefer Yetzirah* and the *Zohar* incorporate an astrological approach into the cosmology they describe. The *Zohar* states:

I have found in the books of the ancients a mystical doctrine, and next to it another mystical doctrine, both being in essence one and the same. It amounts to the following. There is a period when the moon is defective, judgment being visited upon her, and the sun being concealed from her. Now it is the moon that at all times and seasons releases souls to enter the sons of men ... But these souls which the moon sends forth when she is in the

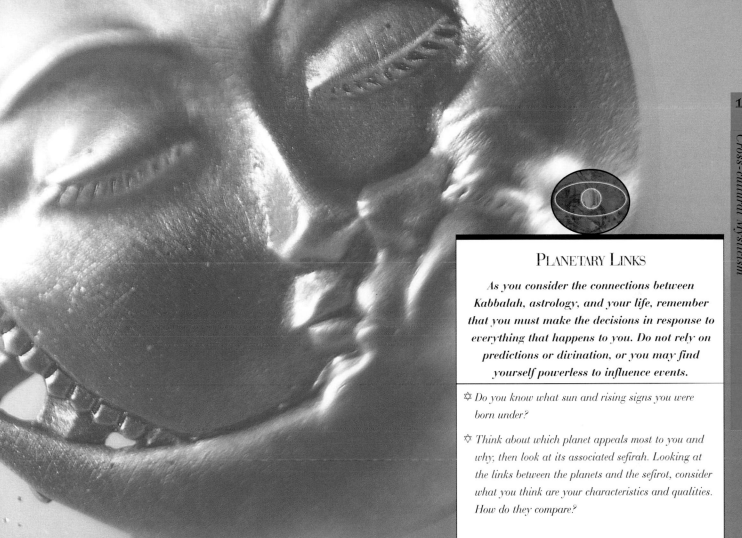

PLANETARY LINKS

As you consider the connections between Kabbalah, astrology, and your life, remember that you must make the decisions in response to everything that happens to you. Do not rely on predictions or divination, or you may find yourself powerless to influence events.

✡ *Do you know what sun and rising signs you were born under?*

✡ *Think about which planet appeals most to you and why, then look at its associated sefirah. Looking at the links between the planets and the sefirot, consider what you think are your characteristics and qualities. How do they compare?*

*grade of completeness, and the perennially flowing stream plays about her, are destined to enjoy abundance of all good things ... and all on account of the allotment (*mazal, or fortune*) that flowed forth and joined itself to that grade in order to be perfected and blessed by it.*

ZOHAR, VAYESHEV, 180B–181A

The word *mazal*, used by Jews today as an expression of congratulations and good luck (*mazal tov*), is connected to the Kabbalistic understanding of the fortune that is allotted by the stars and planets. The related word *mazalot* means "zodiac." From the creation of the lights on the fourth day in Beriah, the zodiac was seen to have dominion over day and night, and influence

life below on Earth. The *Sefer Yetzirah* gives Kabbalists a precise account of the time of year and the area of the human body which the zodiac signs govern, and allots to each of them one of the twelve tribes of Israel. Each sign is said to represent one of the twelve types of human being—a view that continues to hold popularity in mainstream contemporary Western culture.

▲ SUN AND MOON
Each sefirah has a planet associated with it. Until the modern age, only six planets were known, and the Sun and Moon were included as planetary bodies.

CHAPTER SIX

BRINGING KABBALAH INTO YOUR LIFE

The sacred knowledge of Kabbalah is intended to be used in daily life. Meditation, chanting, creativity, and study are some of the routes to greater awareness. Kabbalah is not for dabblers. The exercises in this chapter require honesty and integrity. Use them to create unity within the four worlds of your existence.

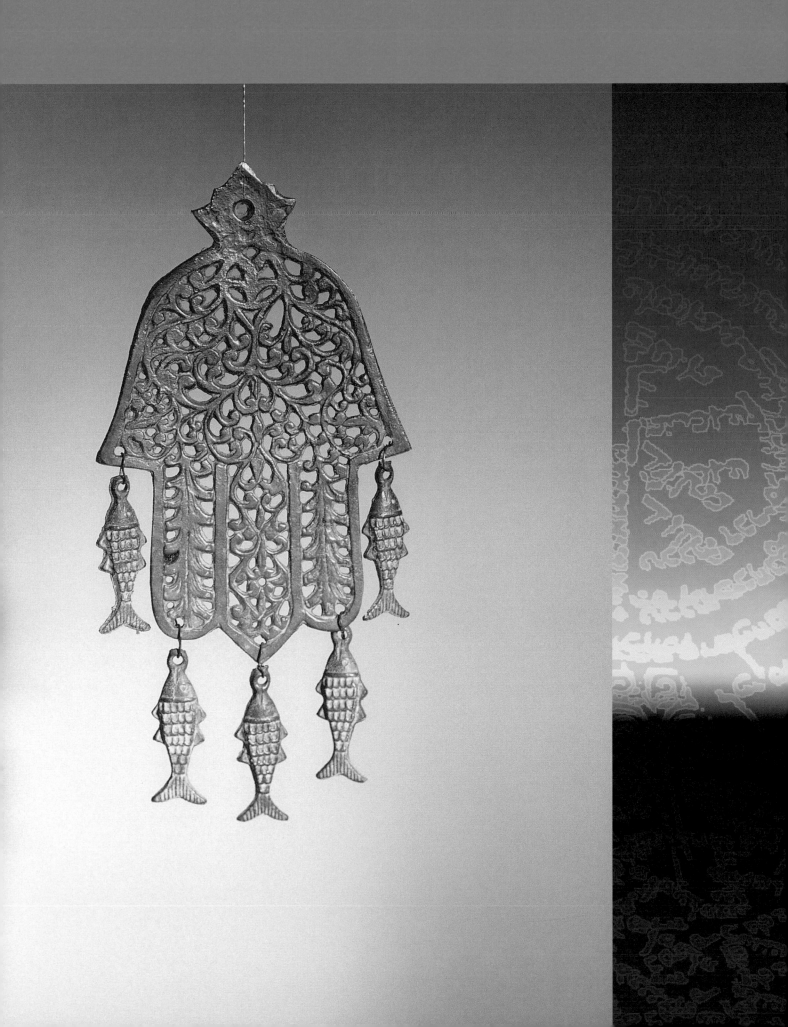

RESTRUCTURING YOUR PERCEPTIONS

In order to see the world differently, you must look differently. This means restructuring your perceptions through the exercise of attentiveness. While it may seem that you see with your eyes, in fact it is the brain that decodes the visual stimuli and turns them into meaningful images. You will need a special notebook to keep a record of your progress. Spend some time selecting a book that you will enjoy using every day.

▼ ESSENCE OF LIFE

Crystals of widely diverse shapes have regularly ordered molecular structures. Seeing the world differently means sometimes looking beneath the surface to recognize structure and essence.

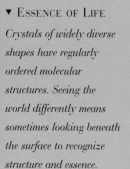

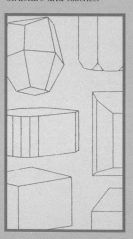

EXERCISE 1

LEARNING TO SEE

This exercise will help you restructure the way you see and interpret your everyday experiences.

1 Go outside and look at a butterfly. Write down what you see as accurately as you can, drawing it if you like. Note down any other thoughts about the butterfly.

2 Answer the following questions to understand more clearly how you see. There are no right answers.

✡ Do you focus on physical characteristics, such as form, color, pattern, and movement?

✡ Do the stages of development (egg, caterpillar, or chrysalis) come into your mind?

✡ Do you think about its beauty, grace, speed?

✡ Are you struck by intangible ideas such as freedom, mortality, or the inter-relationships between the parts of the natural world?

✡ Are you moved by its beauty as a reflection of the miracles of creation in harmony with nature?

✡ Did you experience a fleeting desire to crush or destroy the butterfly, aware of your power over it?

✡ Do you see the butterfly as a gift or expression of love?

✡ Does mystery or awe come to mind—the mystery of creation or the connection between the vast universe and the apparent insignificance of one butterfly?

All these questions address aspects of the Tree of Life:

STRUCTURE AND FUNCTION represent Malkhut and the world of Assiyah.

FORMATION AND DEVELOPMENT represent Yesod and the world of Yetzirah.

SPLENDOR AND MAJESTY represent Hod and Netzach, balanced by endurance and permanence.

BEAUTY represents Tiferet as a reflection of Divine glory and will; it also links the worlds of Yetzirah and Beriah.

POWER AND JUDGMENT represent Gevurah.

MERCY AND LOVE represent Chesed.

WISDOM AND UNDERSTANDING represent Chokhmah and Binah, approaching the world of Atzilut.

Repeat the exercise with a tree, or with a piece of coal, a diamond, or the point of your pencil (the latter three are forms of the same element, carbon). Practice looking and seeing for ten minutes every day, at home, at work, with people, or alone. Repeat for three days so that your new skills are completely absorbed.

EXERCISE 2

RECOGNIZING YOUR CHOICES

Every day you encounter situations in which you have to make choices that have a subsequent impact on your life or the life of people around you. Jewish tradition teaches that every person has within him or her both the inclination to good (*yetzer hatov*) and the inclination to evil (*yetzer hara*). These are represented by angels sitting on each shoulder. Another way of thinking about this idea is the tension between the left and right pillars of the sefirotic Tree, particularly at the positions of Gevurah and Chesed.

1 Make a list of all the choices you have made today, from those you consider the least significant to the most important. This may take some time.

2 Now, thinking back over the same day, note down if there were points at which you thought that you had no choice and had to do or say something because of forces outside and stronger than yourself.

3 Compare the two lists. Think about which is longer and why that might be. Consider whether these two lists are representative of your experience of life.

4 How often do your choices reflect your own desire or need to control and judge (Gevurah)? How often do they express your need to love and show compassion (Chesed)? Alternatively, do you find that your choices reflect an inability to make judgments or express your power in a situation (deficiency of Gevurah)? Do you find yourself incapable of openly offering love and reaching out to others (deficiency of Chesed)?

5 Do your choices reflect a concern with expediency or getting the job done (Malkhut), a need to satisfy your ego (Yesod), a sense that your self and your choices are linked to a higher purpose (Tiferet), or a feeling that you are guided by a higher pure power in what you do (Keter)?

6 Consider a particularly difficult choice that you have to make now or in the near future. Write down what you think are all the options. Then, using the structure of the sefirotic Tree, decide which options represent the sefirot that are strongest and weakest within you. Does looking at the sefirot bring up the possibility of any other choices? Be totally honest with yourself and decide if you are motivated by the good or evil inclination. Remember that *yetzer hara* can be anything that is to the detriment of integrity or the well-being of self, others, or the world.

▶ NATURE'S WAY

Everything we see is caught in a moment of time.

The beautiful butterfly is only a part of the cycle that passes from egg through caterpillar and chrysalis to the extraordinary and delicate adult form. Sometimes we see only a part of what is in front of us. Learn to look beyond the limitations of the moment and perceive the beauty waiting to be seen.

KAVANNAH
in YOUR LIFE

Kabbalah teaches that there should be a kavannah, or focused intention, underlying every thought, prayer, and action. Over the centuries, rituals and meditations developed to accompany every daily action, designed to heighten awareness and ascend to the higher realms of the Tree of Life.

▼ STAY FOCUSED
You may need to create for yourself a written form of kavannah, perhaps a phrase or picture that will remind you of your intention to live with consciousness. You can carry it with you and refer to it if you find yourself drifting.

EXERCISE 3

CREATING A DAILY KAVANNAH

In order to be effective, a kavannah exercise must lift a routine activity into consciousness with a pure intention. For this exercise, you will need to use your new powers of will and concentration, and to be open to a whole range of possible awarenesses.

1 Make a list of every action you do from the moment you wake up until you leave the house in the morning. How many do you think about before or while doing them? Consider what would be the result of not doing each of these acts.

2 Plan your day to allow yourself an extra hour in the morning to do this exercise for the first time. Don't worry, it won't always take so long. Once you have integrated the kavannot (plural of kavannah) into your daily practice, you may only need a few minutes.

3 Using the following list as an example, create your own kavannah as a meditation, chant, phrase, or action:
✡ Waking up—when you open your eyes, look around and give thanks for your life and your ability to wake refreshed. This may be in the form of a chant, a song, or a repeated phrase such as "Thank you for my life."
✡ Getting out of bed—as you arise, be aware of your limbs and your spine working properly to enable you to move. Acknowledge the workings of your body—for

example, reach up with each arm toward the ceiling, looking upward; stretch each leg forward and backward; rotate your head slowly around in a circle, staying aware of all that you see; bend at the waist and stretch downward, looking down.
✡ Using the lavatory—as you attend to the call of nature, give thanks that your body's channels and openings work as they should, opening and closing at the right moment; e.g., you might accompany excretion with a loud chanted "aah." Don't worry about the neighbors.
✡ Washing—as you wash your hands, face, and body, imagine the layers of dead cells, dirt, and germs being rinsed away and the refreshed and clean skin you emerge with. Acknowledge your essential purity with a spoken or sung phrase before and after washing, e.g., "I am pure and clean." Alternatively, slowly clap your wet hands together three times and feel your skin interact with the water.
✡ Getting dressed—before selecting what to wear, think about what qualities of your nature you wish to express. Choose colors and styles that reflect what you need, considering the attributes of the sefirot: blue, Malkhut;

▶ ONE IN A MILLION
Every cloud is unique and yet also lends itself to different images in the mind of those who see it. Part of the task of creating a kavannah for daily practice is to learn to notice and appreciate the small differences in everything and everyone you encounter. This will help you to lift routine activities into conscious awareness.

orange or black, Yesod; dark pink, Hod; light pink, Netzach; yellow and purple, Tiferet; red and gold, Gevurah; white and silver, Chesed; yellow and green, Binah; and a garment that includes all colors for Chokhmah. Before putting on your clothes, wave them above and around your head and visualize that you are enveloping yourself in the sefirotic qualities.

✿ Eating breakfast—before you put any food into your mouth, acknowledge the origins of that food and the people and animals that worked to enable you to eat it. Go through in your mind the processes and steps that brought the food to you. Give thanks for the interrelatedness of all beings and the food chain, e.g., speak aloud your thanks for each stage.

✿ Leaving the house—as you pass through the threshold, look back at your home and acknowledge the safety and comfort it affords you. Touch the doorpost of your home and listen for a moment to the sounds from outside and to your inner voice. Imagine, before you step outside, the oneness of everything, uniting your inner

life with the world around you.

✿ Stepping into the world—look around at your familiar surroundings and try to see them with a new eye. For example, using first your right and then your left arm, make an arc with each, starting with your hand on your heart and stretching it out until it is extended shoulder high, pointing to the side. Then imagine yourself hugging the wondrous creations of the world.

As you become used to this exercise, extend it to include more parts of your day, such as traveling, arriving at work or school, meeting and being with friends and colleagues, enjoying leisure activities, before and after lovemaking, and preparing for bed.

THOUGHT, CREATION, FORMATION, and ACTION

The Kabbalistic four worlds are based on a biblical text from Isaiah and the first verses of Genesis. The Kabbalists stated that before there was anything, there was Divine thought and will. That will brought into creation the universe, which began to take form, differentiate into various structures and processes, and at last became capable of action. We can emulate this process in our own life, and understand ourselves better as a result.

You are created in the image of the Divine Creator, and thus you too function in the framework of these four worlds. Imagine how your life and the world might be if your every action were the result of inspired thought, brought into being by using your own will and talents.

THE THIRTY-SIX

There is a Chasidic tradition that the fate of the world rests, at any one time, on thirty-six righteous people. They may be anyone, and they are not aware that they are one of these crucial people. The lesson here is that any of us may be one of the thirty-six, and therefore we must each act as if we were, for the fate of the world may rest upon us. Furthermore, we must treat every other person as if she or he were one of the righteous ones too, as our actions may influence theirs. Given this possibility, our every action takes on new meaning and importance.

EXERCISE 4

MAKING EVERY ACTION A REFLECTION OF DIVINE WILL

Remember that you are unique and special. With a commitment to sincere spiritual growth, you can use this uniqueness and make every action a manifestation of the strength of the four worlds.

1 Consider an important action that you did in the past week. Write down a description of what you did, how it came about and why you did it. Do not read the rest of this exercise until you have finished writing.

2 Now examine the details of your action and decide whether it was an example of good or evil inclination. Be honest. Decide whether it reflects the left, receptive, reasoning pillar of severity or the right, active, intuitive pillar of mercy of the Tree of Life. See if it is an expression of one or more of the sefirot. Is this typical of your behavior?

3 Now decide what was at the foundation of your action. This goes beyond the details you have already written.

◀ BEAUTIFUL EARTH

The striking green and blue of our planet reminds us of the gift we have been given. Just as God's will created the Earth, so we must take care of everything we create and make it an expression of good. The future of the Earth depends on us.

Try to address universal principles and see if there are issues larger than yourself at work.

4 Consider these aspects of the four worlds: physical behavior, emotion, intellect, and spirit. Does your action reflect one or more of these worlds? How might it have been different if you had involved the other worlds in the act?

5 Try now to go beyond your ego and personal circumstances. Imagine what a Divine will might have wanted you to do. Does it make any difference if Divine will inspires your action?

Think about the next few days ahead. Instead of focusing on the actions to be taken, try to start from the world of Atzilut (Nearness). Consider that there is a primal will that emanates from Ayn Sof, and that you and your life are a unique expression of it. As you encounter people and situations, ask yourself what kind of creation the sacred Creator would want from you; what are your own special talents that make your creations or actions unique?

As you manifest the creative will in the real world, be aware that your uniqueness creates a particular form that will impact on the world. Therefore, you must take great care that every one of your actions is the result of attention to the four worlds and to the possibility that what you do can change the world.

▲ LESSON OF "THE THIRTY-SIX"

Lost in a crowd like pins in a cushion, the legend of the thirty-six righteous people tells that within every generation there are individuals who have a special positive effect on society. Their role is unknown even to themselves, and the story teaches us that we must treat every one of our actions as if the world depended on it.

PERSONAL MEDITATION

There are as many forms of meditation as there are spiritual traditions. Within Kabbalah, meditation practices arise from centuries of development and form part of what is known as practical Kabbalah. They can be intellectual, emotional, or physical.

▶ MEDITATION AID
Mandalas are a traditional mediation aid, composed of concentric diagrams of spiritual significance. They are common within Tibetan Buddhism, where deities are alotted set positions. The four corners represent the world, and thus the totality of existence, showing clear parallels with Kabbalah.

SELF-ISOLATION

After *hagah*, *hitboddedut*, or self-isolation, is a second type of Kabbalistic meditation. It is an internally directed technique and requires not only physical isolation but also isolating the mind from external stimuli. Kabbalist Chaim Vital instructed that, to do this, one must separate soul from body, so that the sense of physical self disappears. However, he warned that this practice is highly dangerous and should only be attempted after years of study and experience.

EXERCISE 5

MEDITATING WITH REPETITION

Hebrew scriptures commonly refer to *hagah*, which are words or phrases repeated over an extended time. Kabbalistic meditation uses this technique, combining vowels, consonants, or words as its raw material. This exercise uses a similar method to elevate your spiritual self.

1 From the Bible or chapters in this book on the sefirot and the paths, choose one or more words that are particularly powerful for you. Form them into a phrase, which may be in English, Hebrew, or any other language that you speak fluently, or a combination.

2 Find a quiet, comfortable space and choose a time when you will not be disturbed. To begin with, set a timer for ten minutes, gradually increasing your session to a half-hour as you become more adept. Sit on a chair or on the floor, with your back straight and your eyes almost shut, so that you can see only the floor below.

3 Start by taking several deep breaths, in through the nose and out through the mouth. You may exhale with a voiced sound or sigh to dispel pent-up energy. Acknowledge the Divine power that guides you and helps you to maintain a pure intent. Then begin to chant the phrase you have chosen, until you have connected the rhythm of the phrase to your breathing. Continue until the end of the set time.

4 Before rising, again acknowledge and thank the Divine power that guides and protects you.

EXERCISE 6

CONTEMPLATING TEXTS TO REPAIR YOURSELF

This exercise lets you use existing texts as a basis for contemplation.

1 From the Bible or any other book that has been significant in your life, choose a short extract that speaks to you on a spiritual, intellectual, and emotional level, i.e., one that makes you feel, think, and sense something of great importance about reality. You may wish to copy it onto a sheet of paper to focus your attention.

2 Do step 2 from Exercise 5, keeping your eyes open.

3 Before reading, acknowledge the Higher Power that guides you with pure motives and integrity. Slowly read the text aloud, pausing to give yourself time to think. Then read it again, either aloud or silently.

4 Spend the remainder of the time contemplating the text. You may or may not wish to refer to it again. Allow your thoughts to flow from the words, ideas, and feelings. If you find you have drifted away, look again at the text. Consider how the wisdom contained in the text can help you in your life at this time.

5 At the end of the time, re-read the text slowly aloud and give thanks for the guidance and protection of the Higher Power that surrounds you. You may wish to write down your observations and points of action.

EXERCISE 7

ISOLATING THE MIND

Nachman of Bratslav adapted *hitboddedut* into an accessible form, which you can learn here.

1 Go into an undisturbed setting where you will not be distracted. At first you may need to set a timer for ten minutes. Sit or lie down and keep your eyes almost closed, but not completely.

2 Acknowledge the Higher Power that protects and guides your pure intention. Take several deep, clearing breaths and allow your body to relax.

3 Imagine that you are watching or listening to your own mind as a detached observer. Observe your thoughts.

4 At the end of the meditation, give thanks for your capacity to discern, then write down any observations.

◄ EYES CLOSED
This Hindu monk closes his eyes and puts his hands together to facilitate meditation. Use whatever techniques you prefer to achieve a state of calm.

THE POWER *of* DIVINE NAMES

Names have power in many cultures. As we have seen, each sefi-rah is associated with one of the many names of God. In Jewish tradition, many practices have arisen linked to the various names, each recognizing an aspect of Divinity that connects both to the universe and to the individual.

▶ABULAFIA'S MANDALA
These circles were created by the thirteenth-century Kabbalist Abraham Abulafia. They contain different combinations of Hebrew letters and Divine names. These were to be repeated over and over in order to transcend rational thought and touch the higher realms.

RABBINICAL WARNING

The rabbis feared the uncontrollable power of these names, and always warned that such practices be protected with particular rituals, such as the ashes of the red heifer (Numbers 19), and by studying with a learned and balanced teacher.

Only one who believes in the ever-present real-ity of God can engage in the practice of using names of God for meditation or spiritual growth. This is an *a priori* assumption of Kabbalists, for whom God is at the center of being. It is not for dabblers, nor for those with a generalized, unde-fined sense of spirituality. Such people risk their sanity and their lives.

אלהים ELOHIM: GOD THE CREATOR

The name of the Creator throughout the first chapter of Genesis is Elohim, which is a plural form literally meaning gods. In this premonotheis-tic period, it is likely that the name was influenced by the surrounding polytheistic cultures. Some academic biblical scholarship assigns the use of different names of God to various redactors: E was the source who used Elohim, while J was the source who used YHVH.

Elohim is placed at the head of the left pillar of justice, as the source of law. It was seen by Isaac Luria as a numerical representation of the sefirot:

א alef = E, the crown or skull of Keter;

ל lamed = L, the three mentalities of Chokhmah, Binah, and Da'at;

ה hay = H, the five corners of the human being: Chesed, Gevurah, Tiferet, Netzach, and Hod;

י yod = Y, Yesod;

ם final mem = M, Malkhut.

This word appears several times in the sefirotic Tree of Life, associated with Binah, with YHVH in Tiferet, and with Tzva'ot (Hosts) in Hod.

יהוה YHVH: The Tetragrammaton

The name YHVH first appears in Genesis 2:4, linked with Elohim. The Creator God later takes on additional qualities and becomes the God who was revealed to Moses in the burning bush. The word itself is part of the ineffable mystery. It is formed from the letters of the verb *to be* and implies future, present, and past. At some point it came to be pronounced and thought of as the word *Adonai* (My Lord). The essence of the name is Eternal Being and this word is placed on the right pillar of mercy on the Tree of Life. Adonai was so given this pronunciation so that unwary people would not try to pronounce the Divine name.

Medieval Kabbalists Eliezer Rokeach and Isaac Luria interpreted the permutation of the letters YHVH in a mathematical array that led to the concept of the 231 gates (see pages 56–57).

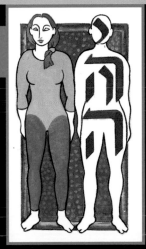

EXERCISE 8

YOU ARE MADE IN THE IMAGE OF YHVH

It is possible to experience the power of YHVH in your life, using this following exercise.

Look at the inscription of the word YHVH on this page. It is composed of four Hebrew letters set on a white background, and is written vertically from the top:

י the letter *yod* representing the world of Atzilut (Nearness) and the Divine Will;

ה the letter *hay* representing the world of Beriah (Creation) and the intellect;

ו the letter *vav* representing the world of Yetzirah (Formation) and emotion;

ה the letter *hay* representing the sefirah of Malkhut (Kingdom) and the world of Assiyah (Action).

1 Visualize the three vertical lines formed by the stacked letters of YHVH as the pillars on the Tree of Life: the left pillar of severity (restriction); the central pillar of will; and the right pillar of mercy (expansion). Memorize the shape of the individual letters, using the reference above.

2 Now stand up with your feet hip-width apart. If you have a full-length mirror, you can see that you are formed in the image of the vertical letters YHVH. If not, use the inscription to remind you and to help you imagine this image.

3 Half-close your eyes and, using your hands or imagining a Divine presence in your mind's eye, trace the Hebrew letters in front of your body: at the top, the let- ter *yod* is located at your head, the crown of Keter; next down, the letter *hay* is located at your shoulders, arms, and hands; they are the understanding of Binah, the discernment and strength of Gevurah, the wisdom of Chokhmah, and the mercy and lov- ing-kindness of Chesed; the letter *vav* is located at your spine, linking to Keter with the knowledge of Da'at, the beauty of Tiferet, the foundations of Yesod, and the in-dwelling presence of the Shekhinah in Malkhut; the letter *hay* is located at your hips, legs, and feet, connecting with the glory and rever- beration of Hod, the endurance and victory of Netzach, and the sexual life force of Yesod.

4 Repeat aloud as you trace the letters over your body, "I am made in the image of God." Allow this realization to penetrate your spirit, mind, feelings, and body. Observe how this affects you.

5 At the end of this meditation, acknowledge the Higher Power that gives you your being and connects you to the infinite source of life.

6 Write down your observations. You may be inspired to draw, dance, sing, or create something new with your hands. Do it.

CHANGING YOUR APPROACH

A good teacher once said to me, "If you always do what you've always done, you'll always get what you've always got." Anyone who has ever wished for a lifestyle change, from weight loss to career advancement, or even the Nobel Prize, will recognize the truth and significance of this simple statement. Most people become creatures of habit, and the needs of everyday life often impede one's attempts to change.

Kabbalah, like other spiritual disciplines, requires a commitment to change and a letting go of fixed ways of being and acting. In order to repair oneself and the world, it may be necessary to face fears, let go of cherished ways and attitudes, change direction, take on new practices. You will discover what is asked of you as you progress in the study of Kabbalah.

OUR DAILY BREAD

The most accessible arena for personal change is your daily routine. Some of the preceding exercises will have helped you to understand how spiritual practice can be integrated into daily life. If your intention is to live a life of physical, emotional, intellectual, and spiritual integrity, then some things will have to change.

1 Begin with the food you eat every day. Think for a moment, and notice the first things that occur to you about your food and drink habits. Jot down these observations in your notebook.

2 Now consider the source of your food, the conditions under which it is produced, the people who are responsible for producing it and getting it to you. What are the principles underlying the production of the food you eat? Do you see integrity and a balance between Gevurah and Chesed?

3 Make an effort to find out which companies produce your food and what their policies are. Do they measure up to your sense of integrity? Let the understanding of Binah and the wisdom of Chokhmah guide you in your choice of what you buy.

4 Be aware that everything that you put into your mouth either brings you closer toward unity with the Divine good or takes you further away from it. Make a commitment to eat and drink with greater consciousness and begin by deciding what changes you need to make in your grocery shopping. Allow the indwelling presence of the Shekhinah to guide you when you make your shopping list or choose a restaurant.

5 Once you sit down to eat, allow time to acknowledge the source of your food and its connection to the Earth. Give thanks before and after eating; you are what you eat, so enable your body to become an expression of balance between the sefirot. Share your food with strangers and those in need; let the energy of Chesed be manifested in your generosity of spirit. Take time to prepare and present food with love and beauty, so that the energies of Hod and Tiferet can resonate within and around you.

6 Once you have used this approach for your food, begin to think about what you wear and the products that you use every day, where you choose to go for your vacation, and what organizations you support. Aim to make every aspect of your life an expression of conscious devotion to what you know is right.

The prophet Micah said, "God has told you what is good and what the Eternal asks of you. Is it not to do justice [Gevurah], to love mercy [Chesed], and to walk humbly with your God [Malkhut]."

MICAH 6:8

Only by establishing a congruent way of living, with your thoughts and feelings matched in outer actions, can you progress along whatever spiritual path you are following.

◀ FOOD FOR LIFE
The food you eat becomes you. Consider the source of your food and the ethics of those who produce it. Food preparation can be an expression of love or of carelessness—think about which of these traits you would prefer in your life.

Inner Healing

At the end of his life, Moses spoke to all the children of Israel, summarizing God's teaching and promises to them. After forty years of wandering in the physical wilderness, the people were deemed ready to take on the responsibility for their spiritual health. At the heart of it all is love, the love of God and the choice of life and good over death and evil.

Healing of body, heart, mind, and spirit is referred to often in the later books of the prophets. Malachi's vision clearly associates the attributes of Keter and Shekhinah:

> *The sun of righteousness shall arise with*
>
> *healing in its wings.*
>
> MALACHI 3:20

Almost every aspect of our lives today reflects the interplay between the personal, the communal, and the global. The mechanical and biochemical innovations that have improved the quality of our lives have also created the threatening reality of social and environmental apocalypse. Only human will and action can heal our world.

▶ JESUS HEALS

As Jesus heals the mother-in-law of Peter, the Divine energy of love passes to the sick woman. The gift of healing can be used to cure both physical sickness and ills of the mind and soul.

SPIRITUAL PARALLELS

Faith healers of the Christian tradition believe that they are conduits for healing energy that comes directly from God. They cite Jesus' healing ministry and the gift of grace of the New Testament as their justification.

EXERCISE 10

HEALING THROUGH LOVE

The Hebrew word for love, *ahavah*, has many healing possibilities. Consider the structure of the word:

א the letter *alef* is the mother letter of breath, with a Hebrew numerical value of 1;

ה the letter *hay* is an elemental letter signifying the spirit of God, with a numerical value of 5;

ב letter *bet (vet)* is one of the seven double letters, signifying the goodness of the light created by God, with a numerical value of 2;

ה the letter *hay* is as above, with a value of 5. The word has a total numerical value of 13.

1 Say the Hebrew word *ahavah* (aah-haa-vaah) until you are comfortable with it. You may wish to say it all on one note or by varying the notes.

2 Stand with your legs hip-width apart; do this in a secluded but open space. Open up to the possibility of healing your body, mind, and spirit by bringing in Divine love and allowing it to flow from you.

3 Facing first to the west, the direction of Yesod, be aware of the healing power of form in balance and slowly chant the word *ahavah* thirteen times. Feel the effect of doing this. Then turn to the east, the direction of Tiferet, and repeat, this time aware of the healing power of beauty. Sense if there is a difference.

4 Now turn to the north, the direction of Gevurah, and acknowledge the healing power of strength and discernment. Again chant *ahavah* thirteen times. Feel the impact. Turn slowly to the south, the place of Chesed, and consider the healing power of mercy and loving-kindness. Repeat the chant. Stand quietly.

5 You have now chanted *ahavah* fifty-two times, which is twice the numerical value of YHVH. Realize that you can receive and give this Divine love at any time.

EXERCISE 11

UNIFYING THE FOUR WORLDS

This exercise helps you create a central prayer space as a focus for meditation.

1 Consider the four elements that represent the four worlds: earth, Assiyah; water, Yetzirah; air, Beriah; fire, Atzilut. Collect some earth, water, and air from places that are important to you. Light a candle to create fire. On a flat surface place the elements in the above order. Alternatively, place the items on four separate shelves or tiers above one another.

2 Contemplate the world around you and think of an aspect in need of healing. This may be social, political, or environmental, but should not be a reflection of your prejudices. Decide what healing is required.

3 Now contemplate the four worlds as symbolized before you. Allow yourself to sense how the Divine will, love, and justice of Atzilut could emanate through Beriah, take form in Yetzirah, and be manifested in Assiyah, where you are, to heal the damage that you identified in the world.

4 Acknowledge that this healing can begin only from you, and decide how you will manifest the first step of the process. Make a commitment to take action.

5 Make notes of what you discovered about yourself and what you will do to begin the healing. Be specific and create a timetable for action.

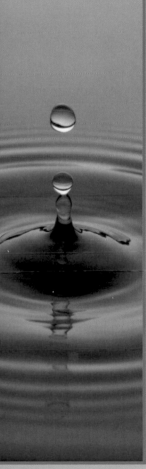

▲DROPLETS OF LIFE

The elements of water, fire, earth, and air represent the forces of nature and the energies of the four worlds. Examine your own life and identify which of these energies you are lacking.

DIRECTING YOUR CREATIVITY

In nature, plants and some animals demonstrate geotropism (orientation toward Earth) or heliotropism (orientation toward the sun), ensuring that their bodies move in the right direction for their development. Similarly, those on the path of spiritual growth and healing must direct themselves toward contemplation, devotion, and action in order to ensure development.

Abraham Isaac Kook, one of the great twentieth-century Kabbalists, said:

*We cannot identify the abundant vitality within all
living beings, from the smallest to the largest, nor the
hidden vitality enfolded within inanimate creation.
Everything constantly flows, vibrates, and aspires. Nor
can we estimate our own inner abundance.
Our inner world is sealed and concealed, linked to a
hidden something, a world that is not our world,
not yet perceived or probed.*

*Everything teems with richness, everything
aspires to ascend and be purified.
Everything sings, celebrates, serves, develops, evolves,
uplifts, aspires to be arranged in oneness.*

OROT HAKODESH 2:374

EXERCISE 12

CREATING A KAVANNAH FOR YOUR CREATIVITY

Whatever your creative interests and talents, you have the capacity to direct that creativity for good. so that it expresses your potential and shares something worthwhile with the world.

1 In your notebook, make three columns. In the first, write down what you think are your creative abilities, leaving plenty of space between them. In the second column, list what you have done with each talent in the past year. In the third column, list what you would like to achieve in the year ahead.

2 Choose one of your creative abilities to work on now. (You may repeat the rest of the exercise with the others.)

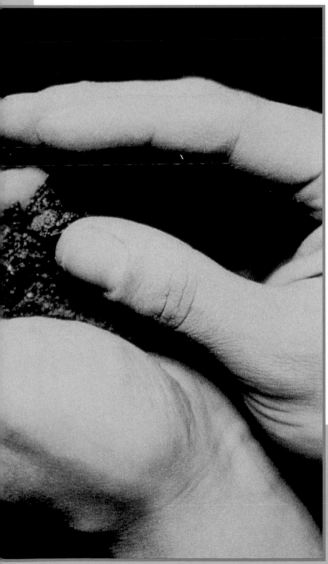

Be certain that your talent is to be used for good. Decide if your creative talent is primarily in the physical, emotional, intellectual, or spiritual world, or a combination. Which of your attributes contribute to your talent? What qualities in you obstruct your talent from expressing its potential? Be honest. Does your underlying intention come from a pure spirit?

3 Looking at what you want to achieve, visualize what would change if you were inspired by a loving light and a will beyond yourself. What new creative possibilities emerge? Now imagine bringing the qualities of each of the sefirot in Yetzirah into being in Assiyah. You may need to refer to the chapter on the sefirot. Consider how the central pillar of will mediates between the expansive pillar of mercy and the receptive/restrictive pillar of justice.

4 Looking at previous chapters, decide which paths and which angels are most relevant to this task, and allow their creative energy to merge with your creative will. Decide what you must give and what you are willing to receive. This may include help, criticism, and judgment from others; assertiveness, receptiveness, strength, or letting go from you.

5 Put away your notebook and sit quietly with your eyes closed. Contemplate your creative process and the results you want to see. Allow the energy of the angels and the sefirot to enter your consciousness.

6 Acknowledge the guidance of the Higher Power and give thanks for your talent. Now begin the work.

◄ CLEAR INTENTIONS
To raise any plant or vegetable, you must have a clear intention, which you develop by preparing the soil, buying the right seeds, tending the plant, watering it neither too much nor too little, protecting it, pinching off excess shoots, and harvesting at the right time. In the same way, your creativity requires a kavannah and attention to detail if it is to take root, blossom, and flourish.

The day is short, and the work is great, and the laborers are sluggish, and the wages are high, and the Master of the house is insistent.

RABBI TARFON

SAYINGS OF THE FATHERS

Seeking Oneness

The Kabbalistic term yichud *(unity or oneness) describes the work of unification between the worlds, in order to come to unity with God. You have already taken the first steps on that path. However, you must not delude yourself that the surface is the essence. As you dig deeper into the earth or dive deeper into the water, the density increases and more and more is packed into the same volume. So it is with Kabbalah.*

God said to Abram (Genesis 12), "Go forth."

God said to Abram, "Go to your self, know your self,

fulfill your self."

ZOHAR 1:78A

This verse is addressed to every person. Search and discover the root of your soul, so that you can fulfill it and restore it to its source, its essence. The more you fulfill yourself, the closer you approach your authentic self.

MOSES ZACUTO (SEVENTEENTH CENTURY)

▶ DEEP IN PRAYER

These Jewish men are engaged in daily prayer at the Western Wall, the remnant of the Temple, in Jerusalem. Their devotion, as with all who pray, brings them closer to the Divine and helps guide their daily behavior.

MOMENTS OF ENLIGHTENMENT

Perhaps you have had a moment in your life when you experienced God, or the Divine light, or suddenly understood the power and meaning in the universe. If you have, you know that from that moment, life becomes bigger, more meaningful, and more awesome than is imaginable. All of the work of Kabbalah aims at those moments, bringing the holy into everyday life and raising everyday life into holiness.

▲ DAILY REMINDER
*Prayer beads are a form of
meditation and reminder of
spiritual awareness. Many
traditions use prayer beads
to facilitate religious
practice. The goal is to
unite prayer and spirit, and
bring them into everyday
actions.*

THE THREE TASKS OF KABBALAH

As you have seen, the work of Kabbalah consists of contemplation, devotion, and action. It is better to engage in this work with a companion and a teacher, to keep you grounded and on the right track. In looking for a teacher, be careful to ensure that he or she comes from a position of integrity and commitment, with a deep knowledge of the tradition. There are too many people out there in the marketplace willing to exploit others.

Contemplation involves applying your mind to the study of texts, the metaphysical world, and the teachings of other traditions. It should also include regular meditation, to recognize the teachings that arise in your daily life and link them to Kabbalistic wisdom.

Devotion can be prayer of any form or service of the heart, what Christians call doing God's work. From a position of gratitude and willingness to act out the Divine will, you can make every moment an opportunity for recognizing and acknowledging the presence of love and awe.

Action is manifesting the Divine will from moment to moment in your life. By creating rituals, you can make one or more of the daily things you do into an act of prayer. Similarly, your seemingly mundane actions can be an expression of higher love and light in the world.

CHAPTER SEVEN

GREAT MINDS OF KABBALAH

Kabbalah has been a continuing process of creativity, interpretation, and application since the first century C.E. Scholars and mystics have committed themselves to a life of study and prayer because the reward seemed so great: the possibility of understanding the meaning of existence and the will of God.

The historical information in this chapter gives an overview of the ideas found within this tradition over the past two millennia. Although the first thousand years is shrouded in mystery, each succeeding century has seen the rise of outstanding scholars and teachers of Kabbalah.

100 C.E.   200 C.E.   300 C.E.   400 C.E.   500 C.E.   600 C.E.   700 C.E.   800 C.E.   900 C.E.   1000 C.E.   1100 C.E.   1200 C.E.   1300 C.E.   1400 C.E.   1500 C.E.   1600 C.E.   1700 C.E.   1800 C.E.   1900 C.E.   2000 C.E.

Classic Texts *of* Kabbalah

Early Kabbalistic teachings are intermingled with biblical legend because the Jewish bible was believed to have been transmitted directly from God, providing a strong motivation for mystic interpretation. These early teachings were recorded in key texts which became the basis of ever-expanding mystical commentaries and Kabbalistic theories.

▼ FRENCH SCHOOL
Written by an unknown rabbi of southern France, the Sefer ha-Bahir reinforces the concept of the Tree as spiritual symbol and guiding light, stating that God spoke the following: "It is I who have planted this tree, that all the world may delight in it." This early school of Kabbalah greatly influenced later medieval commentators of Palestine and Spain.

TThe Book of Formation

The *Sefer Yetzirah* (Book of Formation) appeared in the early Rabbinic period, between the second and sixth centuries C.E. It lies at the foundation of Kabbalistic literature, despite the fact that it is less than 3,000 words in length. Though reputed to have been created by Abraham, the Book of Formation was probably written in the early post-biblical period, possibly by the legendary Rabbi Akiva.

This key work establishes a symbolic picture of the universe, based on the sefirot, explaining the relationship between the heavens above and the Earth beneath, or, in modern terms, the macrocosm of God, the angels, and the universe and the microcosm of humanity and life on Earth. Another central aspect of the book is the explanation of the mystical power of the twenty-two Hebrew letters to reveal the secrets of the universe and God. The letters, emanating from the voice and breath of God, form the basis of the rest of creation, including the souls of every human being. The 231 gates are the symbolic points of interaction between the letters. The whole of creation emerged from the one ineffable name of God, which made matter out of the energy (chaos) in the universe. This extract demonstrates the mystical nature of Kabbalistic understanding:

Twenty-two foundation letters: God engraved them [with voice], carved them [with breath], weighed them and transposed them, Alef [the first letter] with them all. And God permuted them, and with them formed [the soul of] all that was ever formed, and [the soul of] all that ever will be formed … and all of them oscillate cyclically. Thus, they emerge through 231 gates, and everything formed and everything said emanates from one Name. From chaos God formed substance, and made that which was not into that which is. God carved great stones out of air that cannot be grasped.

SEFER YETZIRAH 2:2–6

1

◄ LAND OF THE BIBLE

The mystic writings of the rabbinic period, including the Book of Formation, *sought to understand the Divine word of God, handed to the prophet Moses at Mount Sinai. The mountain still exists and is a place of pilgrimage for Jews, Christians, and Moslems.*

ca. 1800 B.C.E.
Migration of Abraham from Ur of Chaldea to Canaan (Israel).

1 **ca. 1300** B.C.E.
Period of the exodus of Children of Israel from Egypt. Giving of the Torah (foundation of the Jewish Bible) at Mount Sinai.

1000–925 B.C.E.
Period of King David and Solomon; possible composition of the first Psalms.

650–585 B.C.E.
Period of the prophecy of Jeremiah.

586–536 B.C.E.
Destruction of the First Temple in Jerusalem and period of exile in Babylonia; period of Daniel in Babylon and Ezekiel's mystical vision of the Merkavah (Chariot).

70 C.E.
Destruction of the Second Temple in Jerusalem by the Romans under Titus.

100–400 C.E.
Composition and codification of the Mishnah and Talmud. The first century of the Common Era saw the period of Rabbi Akiva, presumed author of the *Sefer Yetzirah*, and his student Rabbi Shimon bar Yochai, the first person credited with authorship of the *Zohar*.

THE BOOK OF BRILLIANCE

Kabbalah as a school of thought arose in France with the appearance of *Sefer ha-Bahir* (Book of Brilliance or Brightness) in the second half of the twelfth century in Provence, although it was attributed to Nechuniyah ben Hakanah, who lived in the first century. Through commentaries on passages from the Bible, this little book presents a variety of speculations about the nature of God through the structure of the sefirot, or "lights," the Tree of God, and the existence of Satan and evil as an integral quality within God itself.

1

THE *ZOHAR*

During the later Middle Ages, Jewish mystics adopted new concepts of piety and righteousness. These are expressed in the Zohar, *which is the seminal Kabbalistic work of this period.*

According to legend, Rabbi Shimon bar Yochai, a student of Rabbi Akiva, is credited with the creation of the *Zohar* (Book of Splendor, Enlightenment or Radiance). He is reputed to have written it after the Romans had executed his teacher, Rabbi Akiva. The story goes that he hid with his son Eleazar in a cave for thirteen years to escape the persecution of the Roman emperor. During that time he received knowledge and wisdom direct from God. When they emerged, Rabbi Shimon was so distressed by what he perceived as the absence of spirituality in the Jewish people that he returned to his cave to meditate. There he was told to teach the secret wisdom only to those who were ready to receive it. Sometime after this period, it is likely that an esoteric school developed, whose scholars closely guarded the secrets while cultivating the growing tradition of Kabbalah.

STORIES OF AUTHORSHIP

Scholarship has determined that the *Zohar* emerged between 1280 and 1286 in Spain as the work of Moses de Leon. However, he too made its authorship something of a mystery by claiming that he had discovered an ancient manuscript and copied the midrashim (interpretations of the Torah) originally written by Rabbi Shimon bar Yochai. After his death, however, his wife stated that there was no ancient manuscript, that he had written the work himself and accredited it to Shimon bar Yochai in order to assure its acceptance and financial success.

STRUCTURE AND PURPOSE

The *Zohar* is an enormous collection of commentaries on the Torah (the five books of Moses) and later parts of the Bible, perhaps written over several centuries by numerous scholars. In its original form, as distributed by Moses de Leon, it consisted of poetic and mystical commentary on the Torah and the Books of Ruth, Lamentations,

◄ THE TOLEDO
SYNAGOGUE
The Spanish town of Toledo flourished in the Middle Ages and became a center of Jewish mysticism. The modern-day revival of Kabbalah has seen a resurgence of interest in medieval Spanish Jewry.

and Song of Solomon, written in a form of Aramaic, the ancient language used by the rabbis who wrote the *Talmud*.

Soon after, other books appeared, also in the same mystical style. One of these, the *Ra'ya Mehemna* (The Faithful Shepherd), became incorporated into the body of the *Zohar*. Another, *Tikunei Zohar* (Repairs or Embellishments of the *Zohar*), subsequently appeared as a book in its own right. Other elements of the *Zohar*, as we have it today, are:

✿ *Sifra-di-Tzeniuta* (Book of the Veiled Mystery);

✿ *Sitrei Torah* (Secrets of the Torah), which focuses mainly on angels and the mysteries of the Divine name;

✿ *Ra'ya Mehemna*, including rules of behavior couched in a narrative spoken by Moses;

✿ *Midrash Ha-Ne'elam* (Concealed or Esoteric Interpretation), which uses sacred numerology to explain biblical texts;

✿ *Tosefta* (Additions), fragments containing references to the sefirot;

✿ *Hekhalot* (Halls or Palaces), descriptions of heaven, hell, and the dwellings of the angels;

✿ *Idra Rabbah* and *Idra Tzuta* (the Great Assembly and the Small Assembly).

WHAT DOES THE *ZOHAR* SAY?

The *Zohar* attempts to explain the relationship between God, the universe, and humanity. The purpose of human life, which is God's greatest creation, is to raise the soul through consciousness to union with God. The *Zohar* introduces the Tree of Life, the model of the cosmos and humanity. It explains the sefirot, but in veiled and symbolic language, showing how the Tree of Life offers a path to achieve spiritual enlightenment in a universe in which everything is interconnected.

900 c.e.
Period of Saadia ben Joseph Gaon (ca. 882–942), Egyptian-born Kabbalist, commentator on the *Sefer Yetzirah*, and author of *Doctrines and Opinions*; Donolo Shabbatai (ca. 913–982), **2** Italian Kabbalist and physician, author of *Sefer Chakhmoni*, a commentary on the *Sefer Yetzirah*, that includes a thorough study of astronomy.

3 **1000 c.e.**
Under Moorish rule in Spain, this is the period of Bachya Joseph ibn Pakuda (ca. 1050–1120), author of *Duties of the Heart*; Solomon ibn Gabirol (1021–1056), author of *Keter Malkhut* (Crown of Kingship); Yehuda ha-Levi (1075–1141), author of powerful love poetry based on Kabbalistic teachings.

1100 c.e.
Period of Abraham ben David of Posquieres, France

(1125–1198), commentator on the *Sefer Yetzirah*, and father of Isaac the Blind; Isaac the Blind (1160–1235), in Provence, France, established the term *Kabbalah* for mystic study; Eliezer ben Yehuda Rokeach (1165–1243) in Worms, Germany, author of *The Spice Dealer*, develops practical Kabbalah.

1200 c.e.
Period of Moses ben Nachman (1194–1270), Spanish mystic and physician who introduces mystical interpretation of biblical commentary; Moses ben Shem Tov de Leon (b. 1240) is known as the most likely author of the *Zohar*; Abraham ben Samuel Abulafia (ca. 1240–1290), practical Kabbalist and author of mystic texts. 1240 marks the year 5000 in the Jewish calendar and thus an auspicious start to the new millennium.

▼ BIBLICAL INSPIRATION
As with all Kabbalistic works, the Zohar was inspired by the holy words of the Torah, or Jewish bible. Throughout the ages, this has been hand-written on parchment and carefully rolled into scrolls.

THE GROWTH
of KABBALAH

While mainstream Judaism concerned itself with studying the Torah during the later Middle Ages, separate mystic schools arose throughout Europe. This new breed of mystics drew on Islamic and Christian traditions, mixing them with Jewish concepts of piety and righteousness, to create a way of life that satisfied the religious needs of the people.

EUROPEAN DEVELOPMENT

In both France and Germany, Kabbalah was dominated by pietistic sects, characterized by calmness of spirit and indifference to social persecution. They were driven more by a need to purify the spirit than by a desire to understand the Divine. Devotees of the Merkavah (Chariot) tradition, based on the visions of Ezekiel, continued to develop rituals to facilitate their ascent to higher levels of holiness.

The Spanish city of Gerona became one of the great centers of Kabbalah from the early thirteenth century. However, by the mid-thirteenth century, anti-Jewish feeling was growing, and compulsory debates were held in which Jews were forced to defend their faith against the king's Christian representatives.

SAFED, ISRAEL

Three events helped Safed develop as a new seat of Kabbalistic learning. Firstly, the Spanish Inquisition brought about a radical rethinking and the need for a new center of learning. In 1492 the Jews were expelled from Spain, and many migrated across to North Africa, Italy, and remote parts of the Ottoman Empire. Secondly, in the same year, Columbus discovered the New World, overturning a whole system of knowledge about the Earth. Thirdly, in 1516 the Turks defeated the Mamlukes and gained control of Egypt, Syria, Palestine, and the Arabian peninsula. The new rulers allowed Jews to settle in Palestine; many chose Safed because it was safe and was the site of several holy burial sites of Talmudic scholars.

A major innovation of the Safed Kabbalists was the notion that the hitherto secret wisdom should be open to all. This would enable people to connect with the Shekhinah, the presence of God in

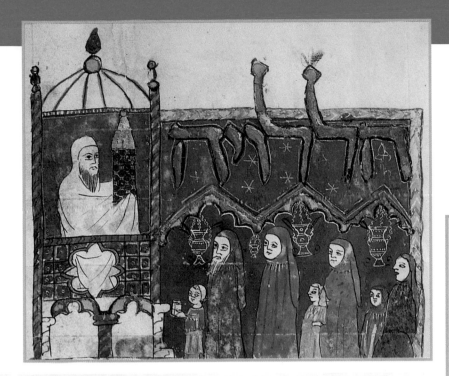

Malkhut, and thus work toward redemption and the repair of the world. Asceticism was seen as one way of purifying oneself for redemption.

THREE GREAT KABBALISTS OF SAFED

The three key Safed mystics were Moses Cordovero, Isaac Luria, and Chaim Vital.

Cordovero founded his own academy in Safed and was responsible for its growth as a center of Kabbalah. His book *Orchard of Pomegranates* systematizes all earlier Kabbalah study.

Isaac Luria, known as the Ari (Lion), developed a new school and divided Kabbalah into separate theoretical and practical disciplines. He used angels and demons to create a practical system to overcome evil and help to hasten the coming of the Messiah. Considered to be a holy man, Luria produced an enormous collection of writings based on the ten sefirot, the four worlds, and the five levels of the soul. Besides his theoretical works, Luria devised a system of meditation using the names of God and meditations with focused intentions using manipulations of Hebrew letters.

Chaim Vital was a disciple of the Ari for two years, and it is thanks to him that we have copies of Luria's work. His *Gates of Holiness* offers many of Luria's teachings and is a complete guide to Kabbalistic meditation.

◄ IMAGE OF A PEOPLE

Although the most serious mystic interpretations were often kept secret, mainstream biblical commentaries were spoken by communal rabbis from the pulpit. This image shows one such sermon, and is taken from the Barcelona Haggadah, ca. 1350. Even after the expulsion of Spanish Jewry in 1492, Kabbalistic writings continued to develop.

1300 C.E.
Period of Menachem Recanati (1350–1440), Italian Kabbalist whose main work, *Perush Al ha-Torah*, a commentary on the Torah, influences the work of Isaac Luria.

1400 C.E.
Period of Isaac Abravanel (1437–1508). Spanish statesman active in Spain, Portugal, and Italy, interprets the Book of Daniel using Kabbalah. Giovanni Pico della Mirandola (1463–1494), establishes a school of Christian Kabbalah in Florence based on the works of Recanati and Plato; Johannes Reuchlin (1455–1522), publishes *On the Miracle-working Name* and *On the Science of the Kabbalah*.

4 1500 C.E.
Safed becomes a major center of Kabbalah: Moses Cordovero (1522–1570) writes *Pardes Rimonim* (Orchard of Pomegranates); German-born Isaac Luria, the Ari or Lion (1534–1572) establishes influential school of Kabbalah; Chaim Vital expands on Luria's teachings; Solomon Alkabetz (1505–1576) establishes Kabbalist center in Salonica.

5 In Prague, Yehuda Loew ben Bezalel (1512–1609) creates the mystic legend of the Golem. In France, Guillaume Postel (1510–1581) translates the *Sefer Yetzirah* into Latin with new commentaries. French mysticism shows the increasing influence of Neoplatonism, Gnosticism, and other philosophies.

► FLORENTINE KABBALAH

Fifteenth-century Florence saw the rise of Christian Kabbalah, which took its inspiration from Jewish, Christian, and secular philosophies of the day.

THE RISE OF CHASIDISM

In the mid-1700s Israel ben Eliezer became known as the Baal Shem Tov, the Master of the Good Name. He founded in Poland the mystical movement known as Chasidism, which within fifty years attracted millions of followers and is today part of both ultra-orthodox sects and the Jewish Renewal movement.

Whereas theoretical Kabbalah had been developed to an almost exalted intellectual level, the Chasidim believed that its teachings were the province of everyone. Meditation, joyous prayer accompanied by singing and dancing, and the love of and communion with nature were integral to Chasidic life. One central aspect of Chasidic practice was hitboddedut, the separation of self from the world for meditation. The Baal Shem Tov rejected the asceticism of earlier Kabbalistic traditions and said, "There is practically no place in the world that is not occupied by God's presence."

He taught that the path to God was much simpler than the way Luria proposed, and that the desire to return to God was enough to consider someone a just person. People needed only to have a pure heart, to believe in God the Creator, and to follow God's teachings joyously. It is not surprising that the movement flourished.

Although the Baal Shem Tov did not want his teachings written down for fear of misinterpretation, they were nevertheless transcribed and appear in *Keter Shem Tov* (Crown of the Good Name) and *Tzavaot di Baal Shem* (Hosts of the Master of the Name).

6

THE TEACHINGS OF NACHMAN

Nachman of Bratslav, the great-grandson of the Baal Shem Tov, grew up as the Chasidic movement was in decline. From his early attraction to asceticism, he grew to a profound and joyous acceptance of the omnipresence and closeness of God. His stories tell of communion with the Divine, not through esoteric books and incantations, but through the delights of nature and human interaction. He said:

When man becomes worthy, to hear the songs of the plants, how each plant speaks in song to God, how beautiful and sweet it is to hear their singing. And therefore it is good indeed to serve God in their midst in solitary wandering over the fields between the growing things and to pour out one's speech before God in truthfulness. All the speech of the fields enters then into your own and intensifies its strength. With every breath you drink in the air of paradise, and when you return home, the world is renewed in your eyes.

Two of his most powerful teachings are:

Man is afraid of things that cannot harm him, and he knows it, and he craves things that cannot be of help to him, and he knows it; but in truth the one thing man is afraid of is within himself, and the one thing he craves is within himself.

There is no obstacle that one cannot overcome, for the obstacle is only there for the sake of the will, and in reality there are no obstacles except in the spirit.

▶ THE CENTER OF CHASIDISM

Chasidic mysticism grew quickly in Poland, which welcomed the positivity of its message. This painting by Bouvine-Frenkel gives a taste of village life in which much of Jewry lived.

◄ DIVERSITY OF RABBINIC THOUGHT

Rabbinic theology became increasingly diverse as Jewry faced the challenges of the Enlightenment, and Kabbalah was shunned by new reformist rabbis as irrational. The challenges of modern life are revealed in this painting by Bouvine-Frenkel, showing a Polish rabbi in traditional garb set against the backdrop of city life.

1600 C.E.
Jacob Boehme interprets Kabbalah with a Christian perspective, and Knorr von Rosenroth (1677–1784) writes *Kabbala Denudata*.

1700 C.E.
In Poland, Israel ben Eliezer, the Baal Shem Tov, (1698 –1760), establishes the Chasidic movement; Moses Chaim Luzzatto (1707–1746), Italian-born Kabbalist, writes *The Path of the Upright*. Also the period of Eliyahu, the Gaon of Vilna, Lithuania (1720–1797), author of eighty Kabbalistic volumes; Nachman of Bratslav (1772–1811), the master of Kabbalistic meditation and author of parables stressing righteous living.

6 1800 C.E.
Jewish theology continues to develop within an increasingly modern world; period of Elijah Guttmacher (1796-1874) in Graetz, Germany, and Judah Alkalai (1798–1878) in Belgrade, Serbia. Jewish nationalism and the Enlightenment movement results in a decline of Kabbalistic practice.

1900 C.E.
In Palestine, the period of Abraham Isaac Kook (1865–1935), the Chief Rabbi of Palestine, poet and mystic; Yehudah Ashlag (1886–1955), translator of the *Zohar* and founder of modern Kabbalah studies, author of *The Study of the Ten Luminous Emanations*; Abraham Joshua Heschel (1907–1972), American conservative philosopher writes *God in Search of Man*; Louis Jacobs (b.1920), English theologian, writes *Chasidic Prayer*; Zalman Schachter-Shalomi (ca. 192?—), American Chasidic teacher establishes the Jewish Renewal movement and writes *The First Step: A Guide for the New Jewish Spirit*.

7 Gershom Scholem serves as professor of Jewish mysticism at the Hebrew University, Jerusalem, between 1935 and 1965.

GLOSSARY

aron: Brother of Moses and Israelite High Priest.

Abraham: The first patriarch, with whom God made the Covenant; father of Isaac.

Abulafia, Abraham: Prophetic Kabbalist of thirteenth-century Spain and Sicily.

Adam Kadmon: Primordial Adam in Atzilut, created as a reflection of God before the creation of the world.

Adonai: the traditional pronunciation of YHVH, meaning "my Lord."

Akiva, Rabbi (ca. 50–135 C.E.): Leader of a theological academy in Bnei Berak; the Romans executed him by flaying for studying the Torah.

Alchemy: The art of transmuting base metals into gold.

Amidah: The standing prayer of eighteen blessings recited three times daily.

Ari, the: Rabbi Isaac Luria (1534–1572), known as the Holy Lion, founder of Lurianic Kabbalah.

Assiyah: Action, the lowest of the four worlds, that of making and doing, where humanity lives.

Astrology: The art of deriving meaning from the study of the positions of stars and planets and the relationship between them.

Atzilut: Nearness to the Divine light, the highest of the four worlds.

Avodah: The service of God, usually translated as *prayer*.

Ayn Sof: The unknowable infinite God, without end.

Baal Shem Tov: Title meaning "master of the good name," Rabbi Israel ben Eliezer (1698–1760), founder of Chasidism in Poland, which enabled ordinary people to reach spiritual heights through joyful prayer, communion with nature, and righteous living.

Bachya ibn Pakuda (ca. 1080–1170): Spanish Kabbalist, author of *Duties of the Heart* and mystical writings.

Bahir (see *Sefer ha-Bahir*).

Beriah: Creation, the second of the four worlds.

Besht

Bezalal: The artist chosen by God in the Torah to create the Tabernacle.

Binah: Understanding, the sefirah at the top of the left pillar.

Brachah: A blessing; from the word, *baruch* meaning blessed.

Buddha: Sidhartha Gautama, the Indian philosopher prince who found enlightenment and became the model for the development of Buddhism.

Chakra: In Yoga, the "wheel," or energy center, through which life force flows.

Chasidism: The mystical Jewish movement that flourished in Poland and Eastern Europe in the eighteenth and nineteenth centuries.

Chesed: Mercy or Loving-kindness, the sefirah in the middle of the right pillar.

Ch'i (ki): Life-force energy.

Chokhmah: Wisdom, the sefirah at the top of the right pillar.

Cordovero, Moses (1522–1570): Kabbalist of Safed's Golden Age, wrote *Or Yakar* (Precious Light) on the *Zohar* and *Pardes Rimmonim* (Orchard of Pomegranates), explaining many Kabbalist concepts.

Crown: The highest chakra, corresponding to Keter in Kabbalah.

Da'at: Knowledge, the non-sefirah on the central pillar mediating between Binah and Chokhmah.

David: Second king of Israel (ca. 1080–970 B.C.E.), who established the capital in Jerusalem.

De Leon, Moses (1250–1305): Spanish Kabbalist author of the *Zohar*.

Deuteronomy: The fifth book of the Torah.

Devekut: Attachment to God through constant acts of consciousness.

DNA: Deoxyribonucleic acid, the building blocks of protein and life.

Ego: Freudian psychological term for the conscious self.

Ehiyeh: "I shall be," part of the name of God associated with Keter.

El: God the creator, name associated with Chesed.

El Shaddai: God of Might, the Divine name associated with Yesod.

Elohim: The first name of God mentioned in Genesis, associated with Binah.

Emanation: The outpouring of Divine light from the higher realms down through the sefirotic Tree of Life.

Enneagram: The "nine-point" geometric representation of cosmic and individual structure, expounded by Georgei Gurdjieff.

Exodus: The second book of the Torah, the story of the Israelites' liberation from slavery in Egypt 1300 B.C.E.

Gavriel: Gabriel, the archangel associated with Yesod in Beriah and the strength of God.

Gematria: The manipulation of numbers and Hebrew letters for meditation and to unlock the secrets of the Torah.

Genesis: The first book of the Torah, the story of creation and the beginnings of the Israelites.

Gevurah: Judgment or Power, the middle sefirah of the left pillar.

Gilgulim: Wheels, as described by Ezekiel in his Chariot Vision.

Gnosis, Gnostics: Second- and third-century C.E. esoteric cult of mystical knowledge, combining teachings from Christianity, Greek theology, Hinduism, and Buddhism.

Great Assembly: The Sanhedrin, the supreme Jewish religious court during the Roman period.

Haniel: Archangel sometimes associated with Netzach.

Hara: The second chakra, linked to life force and survival.

HaShem: "The Name," a respectful substitute for any of the names of God.

Hekhalot: Halls or chambers; a school of mysticism based on the first-century text *Hekhalot Rabbatai* (Great Chambers), which describes meditative methods to enter a mystical state and ascend toward Divine light.

Hitbonnenut: An intellectual form of meditation based on contemplation of texts.

Hod: Reverberation or Splendor, the sefirah at the bottom of the left pillar.

I Ching: The Book of Changes, ancient Chinese teaching based on sixty-four hexagrams that can be used as oracles for divination.

Id: Freudian psychological term for the unconscious instincts and needs of the human mind.

Isaac: The second patriarch, son of Abraham and Sarah, and father of Jacob.

Isaac the Blind (ca. 1200): Spanish Kabbalist who lived in Provence, France.

Isaiah: Eighth-century B.C.E. Hebrew prophet who foretold the Age of the Messiah.

Israel: "The one who wrestles with God"; the name given by God to Jacob after he wrestled with the angel.

Jacob: The third patriarch, son of Isaac and Rebeccah.

Jacob's ladder: Part of Jacob's dream in which he saw a ladder ascending to heaven with angels moving up and down it.

Jerusalem: Capital of Israel and sacred to Judaism, Christianity, and Islam.

Joseph: Son of Jacob and Rachel; he saved the Egyptian and Israelite peoples during a seven-year famine; associated with the sefirah of Yesod.

Joshua: Leader of the Israelites after Moses; he took them into the Promised Land.

Jung, Carl: (1875–1961): Swiss psychiatrist and mystic who expounded the theory of the collective unconscious and linked myth, religion, and dreams.

Kabbalah (often Qabala): From the root meaning "to receive," the mystical tradition of philosophy based on the *Sefer Yetzirah*, *Sefer ha-Bahir*, and the *Zohar*.

Kavannah: Focused intention underlying meditative, religious, and daily practice.

Kelippot: The husks or shells said to have broken at the time of the Creation because of the inability of the Divine vessels to contain the Divine light.

Keter: Crown, the highest sefirah, at the top of the central pillar, associated with the emanation of God's light.

Letters (Hebrew): The *alef-bet* or alphabet of twenty-two letters used to understand the Creation in the *Sefer Yetzirah*.

Leviticus: The third book of the Torah, containing mainly laws.

Luria, Isaac (1534–1572): The Ari, or Holy Lion, founder of Lurianic approach to Kabbalah, based in Safed, Israel.

Maggid of Mezeritch (1704–1772): Dov Baer, one of the great Chassidic masters.

Maimonides (1135–1204): Rabbi Moses ben Maimon, Spanish legalist, physician, and philosopher, one of the greatest of Jewish scholars.

Makom: "Place", one of the Divine names, linked to Jacob's dream.

Malkhut: Kingdom, the sefirah at the bottom of the central pillar, representing the physical world.

Matriarchs: The mothers of the Jewish people—Sarah (Abraham's wife), Rebeccah (Isaac's wife), and Rachel and Leah (Jacob's wives).

Meditation: A spiritual practice involving mental stillness, focus, and sometimes the use of texts or words for contemplation or repetition.

Menorah: Seven-branched candelabrum described in the Torah.

Merkavah: Chariot; the vision of Ezekiel on which the early schools of mysticism were based.

Messiah: The "anointed" one, believed by Jews to be a person or age that will come when the world is set right by the rule of God.

Michael: The archangel at the right hand of God, associated with Tiferet.

Midrash: Explanatory stories or interpretations based on connections between different texts in the Torah and Bible.

Miriam: Sister of Moses and Aaron; emotional leader of the Israelite people after the Exodus from Egypt.

Mishnah: "Teaching by repetition"; the collection of Jewish rabbinic commentaries on the Law from the first two centuries C.E.

Moses: Israel's greatest leader, who led them out of slavery in Egypt and received the Torah from God on Mount Sinai.

Mysticism: Religious or spiritual belief and practice based on intuitive and direct communion with the Divine.

Nachman of Bratslav (1776–1810): Great Chassidic rabbi and teacher, master of meditation and author of many stories.

Nefesh: One of the three levels of soul, the lower soul in human beings.

Neshama: The upper soul, which ascends to the Divine Source.

Netzach: Eternity or victory, the sefirah at the bottom of the right pillar.

Nothingness: Part of the unknowable God, Ayn Sof, which existed before creation and with which Kabbalists aspire to achieve unification.

Numbers: The fourth book of the Torah, telling the story of the Israelites in the wilderness after the Exodus from Egypt.

Otiyot: The letters of the Hebrew alphabet.

Pardes: Orchard, paradise, or garden; also an acronym for an approach to the study of Jewish teachings on four ever deeper levels.

Paths: The connections between the sefirot.

Patriarchs: The fathers of the Jewish people: Abraham, Isaac, and Jacob.

Prophets: Divinely inspired individuals who spoke God's word to the people, e.g. Isaiah, Ezekiel, Jeremiah; also the second part of the Hebrew Bible.

Proverbs, Book of: Biblical book traditionally ascribed to King Solomon, full of moral and ethical maxims and poetry.

Psalms, Book of: Biblical book of songs, ascribed to King David and others, containing songs of praise and petitions to God.

Qabalah (See Kabbalah).

Rafael: The archangel of healing, associated with the sefirah of Hod.

Reincarnation: In Jewish mysticism, the belief that after death the human soul may live again in another person.

Ruach: Literally "wind"; the middle soul, which supports the Throne.

Safed (also Tzfat, Zfat): Town in northern Israel that was the center of Kabbalistic study and creativity in the sixteenth and seventeenth centuries.

Samael: The angel also known as Satan, God's poisoner, associated with the sefirah of Gevurah and cosmic evil.

Sandalphon: The angel associated with the sefirah of Malkhut.

Sefer ha-Bahir: The Book of Brilliance, one of the earliest Kabbalistic texts, which discusses the sefirot and reincarnation. Also known as *Sefer Bahir* and also *Bahir*.

Sefer Yetzirah: The Book of Formation, one of the essential works of Kabbalah, attributed to Rabbi Akiva.

Sefirah, Sefirotic: Divine emanations or attributes of God to direct the universe; spheres of Divine energy.

Shabbat (Sabbath): The seventh day, a day of rest, because God rested from the work of Creation on the seventh day.

Shekhinah: The indwelling presence and feminine aspect of God, represented in the sefirah of Malkhut.

Shema: "Hear"; the first word of the central statement of Jewish belief in the oneness of God.

Sofia: Wisdom, from Greek tradition.

Solomon: Son of David and third king of Israel, builder of the Temple and putative author of Song of Songs and the Book of Proverbs, and Ecclesiastes.

Soul: The essence of the human being, created and given by God, which aspires to ascend to reunification with the Divine.

Sparks: The fragments of the Divine vessels that shattered at Creation and fell from Atzilut to Beriah.

Sufism: Islamic mystical tradition.

Superego: Freudian psychological term referring to the conscience, the sense of right and wrong.

Talmud: Jewish law and tradition compiled in Babylon and Jerusalem, edited between 200 and 600 C.E.

Tetragrammaton: YHVH, the four-letter unpronounceable name of God.

Tiferet: Beauty, the sefirah in the middle of the central pillar.

Tikkun: Repair; a central aspect of the task of Kabbalah, to repair the self and thus reunite the holy sparks and vessels of Divine light.

Tikkun olam: The repair of the world, the duty of all to bring on the messianic age.

Torah: "Teaching" or Law; the first five books of the Bible (Genesis, Exodus, Leviticus, Numbers, and Deuteronomy), the original source of all Jewish belief.

Tree of Knowledge: The tree planted in the Garden of Eden giving knowledge of good and evil, from which Adam and Eve were forbidden to eat.

Tree of Life: The tree of immortality planted in the Garden of Eden next to the Tree of Knowledge; the symbol and schema for the Kabbalistic understanding of the cosmos and all of life, composed of three pillars.

Tzaddik: A righteous person; used to denote a holy Jew who achieves a state of nearness to God through religious and ethical practice.

Tzimtzum: Restriction or contraction; the doctrine that the Divine Creator contracted itself to form a void in which the world could be created.

Unification: (See Yichud).

Uriel: "Light of God," one of the four archangels guarding the heavenly Throne.

Vessels: Containers of Divine light that shattered at Creation, making the sparks that became the stuff of life.

Vital, Rabbi Chaim (1543–1620): Student of Isaac Luria, who recorded his teachings.

Yesod: Foundation, the sefirah near the bottom of the central pillar.

Yetzer ha'tov and yetzer ha'ra: The good and the evil inclinations, two forces acting within every human being.

Yetzirah: Formation, the third of the four worlds, where differentiation takes place.

YHVH: The Tetragrammaton, the unpronounceable four-letter name of God.

Yichud: Unification or oneness, the goal of Kabbalistic study and practice.

Yin and yang: "Dark" and "bright"; the Chinese philosophical concept of two opposing principles that together make up the whole of existence.

Yisrael: (See Israel).

Zadkiel: The archangel associated with the sefirah of Chesed, representing cosmic good.

Zen: "Quiet mind concentration"; Japanese Buddhist meditative practice based on sitting.

Zodiac: The zone across the heavens marking the path of the Sun, the Moon, and the planets, defined by the ancient Greeks.

Zohar: meaning "Splendor," one of the essential books of Kabbalah, attributed to Shimon bar Yochai but probably written by Moses de Leon in the 1280s.

INDEX

A

Aaron 48, 140
Abraham 6, 28, 43, 133, 140
Abraham ben David 135
Abravanel, Isaac 137
Abulafia, Abraham 63, 94–5, 97, *120*, 135, 140
Acher 8
action 116–17, 129
Action (Assiyah) 14, 20, 22–3, 29, 140
Adam 6, *18*, 18, 20, 27, 54, 87
Adam Kadmon 50, 140
Adonai 121, 140
Agrippa of Nettesheim (Cornelius) 13
air 19, 125
Akiva, Rabbi 8, 132, 133, 134, 140
alchemy 102–3, 140
alef 58, 59, 60, 94
Alkabetz, Solomon 137
alphabet 56–79, 94–5, 140
amber 59
Amidah 140
amulets 96
Anatomy of Gold 103
angels 6, 20, 28, 80–9, *80*, *81*, *87*, *89*
    encounters with 88–9
    fallen 86–7
    guardian 86
    hierarchy 82–3
    invoking 86–7
    names 84–5
    on Tree of Life *84*
antithesis 58, 100
Aquarius 79
archangels 20, 85, 87
Aries 72, *73*
Asceticism 137
Ashlag, Yehudah 139
Assiyah 14, 19, 20, 22–3, 29, 140
astrology 90, 108–9
astronomy 90
attentiveness 112–13
Atzilut 14, 15–16, 18, 19, 140
Augustine, St *13*
Avodah 140
ayin 70, 78
Ayn Sof 16–17, 106, *106*, 117, 140
Ayurvedic medicine 102

B

Baal Shem Tov 138, 139, 140
Bachya ibn Pakuda 135, 140
balance 60–1
bells *49*
Ben Azzai 8
Ben Zoma 8
Berg, Rabbi Philip S. 11

Beriah 14, 18–19, 20, 80, 140
bet 66, 94
Bezalal 54, 140
Bible 34, 82, 94, 132, 133
Binah 24, 30, 32, 34, 36, 38–9, 52, 59, 67, 73, 75, 78, 99, 140
black holes 17
Blake, William *19*, *42*, *85*
Boehme, Jacob 13, 139
Book of Brilliance *see Sefer ha-Bahir*
Book of Formation *see Sefer Yetzirah*
Bouvine-Frenkel *139*
Brandwein, Rabbi Yehudah Zvi 11
Buddha *37*, 140
Buddhism 29, 98, 118
    Zen 104–5, 141

C

Carpaccio, Vittore *13*
Chabad 10
Chagall, Marc 7
chakras 64, 98–9, 140
change 122–3
chanting 110
Chariot 83, 92, *93*, 133, 136, 141
Chasidism 116, 138, 140
chayyot 83
cherubim *82*
Chesed 24, 30, 32, 40–1, 42, 66, 68, 75, 78, 79, 87, 99, 140
chet 70, 78, 79
ch'i 103, 106, 140
China 103
Chokhmah 24, 30, 32, 34, 36–7, 38, 52, 66, 72, 74, 75, 78, 140
Christianity 31, 93, 97, 124
    mystics 12–13
consciousness 20
contemplation 129
contraction 17
Cordovero, Moses 137, 140
cosmic consciousness 93
cosmic head *35*
Creation (Beriah) 14, 18–19, 20, 80, 140
creativity 110, 126–7
Crick, Francis 30

D

Da'at 26, 27, 30, 34, 54–5, 99, 140
daily routine 123
dalet 62–3
Darwin, Charles 20
David, King 52–3, 133, 140
Days of Awe 76–7
de Leon, Moses 134, 135, 140
dervishes *101*
Devekut 140

devotion *128*, 129
differentation 20, *21*
DNA 22, 30–1, *31*, 59, *59*, 140
Dogen 104
Dürer, Albrecht 12, *12*

E

earth 19, 125
Earth (planet) 52
eclipse *12*
ego 20, 50, 140
Einstein, Albert *39*
elements 19, 125
Elezier of Worms 86, 94
Elijah 92
elixir of life 102
Elohim 120
Emanation (Atzilut) 14, 15–16, 18, 19, 140
emet 97
emotions 20, *21*
energy, channels of 60–1
enlightenment 128
enneagram 100–1, 140
Enoch 92
Eve *18*, 20, 27
evil 18, 42, 86–7, 93
evolution 20
expansion 17
Ezekiel 59, 83, 92, *93*, 133, 136

F

faith healers 124
fire 16, *17*, 19, 59, 125
Flamel, Nicholas 102
Florence, Italy *137*
Fludd, Robert 13, *84*
Formation (Yetzirah) 14, 18, 19, 20–1
Fourth Way 100
France 136
free will 18

G

Gaon, Saadia ben Joseph 135
Garden of Eden 20, 26
gates 60
Gavriel 85, 88, 97, 140
gematria 94, 96–7, 140
Gemini 74
Germany 136
Gevurah 24, 30, 32, 42–3, 67, 68, 74, 78, 99, 140
gimel 66, 67
Gnosticism 90, 93, 140
God, names 12, 16, 32, 35, 94–5, 96, 120–1, 140
Golem 97, 137
good and evil 42, 86, 93
Great Assembly 140
Gurdjieff, Georgei 100

H

ha-Levi, Yehuda 135
huguh 118
Haniel 85, 140
hay 70, 72
healing 124–5
heart 20
Hebrew, transliteration 13
Hekhalot 82, 92, 135, 140
Helvetius, John Frederick 102
Hermetic Gnostic movement 12
Heschel, Abraham Joshua 139
High Holy Days 76–7
Hinduism 17, 31, 53, 98
hitboddedut 105, 118, 119
hitbonnenut 105, 140
Hod 22, 24, 30, 32, 47, 48–9, 61, 68, 76, 99, 140
Holy Essence 101
human body 98–9

I

I Ching 106, 140
id 50, 140
imbalance 30
immortality 102, 103
India 102–3
intellect 18–19
intentions, focused 114–15
Isaac 6, 43, 140
Isaac the Blind 135, 140
Isaiah 140
Islam 100, 136
Israel 44, 83, 140

J

Jacob 6, 44, 83, 83, 89, 140
Jacobs, Louis 139
Jeremiah 133
Jerusalem 133, 140
Jesse, Tree of 12
Jesus *124*
Joseph 6, 51, 140
Joshua 28, 48, 140
Jung, Carl C. 30, 140
Jupiter 65

K

Kabbalah 140
    beginnings 6
    Christian 12–13
    growth 136–7
    name 6
    present-day study 10–11
    studying 8
Kabbalah Center 10–11
Kaplan, Aryeh 20, 59, 70
kavannah 114–15, 127, 140

kelippot 17, 26, 140
Keter 24, 26, 30, 32, 34–5, 60, 62–3, 72, 73, 99, 110
khaf 68
Kircher, Athanasius 100
knowledge 54–5
Ko Hung 103
koan 105
Kook, Abraham Isaac 126, 139
Koran 85
Krishna 53
kuf 70, 74, 75

L

lamed 70, 76–7
Law of the Octave 100
Law of the Triad 100
Leah 6, 141
letters 56–79, 94–5, 140
Libra 76
light 16, 17, 41
Loew ben Betziel, Yehuda 137
love 41, 93, 96–7, 125
Lubavitch Chasidic movement 10
Luria, Isaac 17, 26, 27, 58, 120, 121, 137, 140–1
Luzzatto, Moses Chaim 139

M

Maat 43
Maggid of Mezeritch 141
Maimonides 141
Malachi 124
Malkhut 24, 26, 30, 32, 37, 49, 52–3, 65, 99, 141
mandalas 118, *120*
Maria Hebraea (Maria the Hebrew) 103
matriarchs 141
Medici family 12
meditation 110, 118–19, 125, 129, 141
mem 58, 61
menorah 141
mercury 102
Mercury (planet) 68
Merkavah (Chariot) 83, 92, *93*, 105, 133, 136, 141
Messiah 141
Metatron, archangel *83*, 85, 92
Micah 123
Michael, archangel 85, 88, 141
midrash 134–5, 141
Miriam 141
Mishnah 133, 141
Moon 62, 64, 66, 67
Moses 6, 28, 28, 34, 37, 46, 48, 121, 124, 141
Moses ben Nachman 135

N

Nachman of Bratslav 119, 138, 139, 141
names, Divine 12, 16, 32, 35, 94–5, 96, 120–1, 140
Native Americans 43

Nearness (Atzilut) 14, 15–16, 18, 19, 140
Nechimiyah ben Hakanah 133
nefesh 101, 141
nervous system 61
neshama 101, 141
Netzach 22, 24, 30, 32, 46–7, 61, 68, 76, 77, 99, 141
Noah 6, 28
Nothingness 16–17, 32, 96, 105, 141
numerology 13, 94–7
nun 70, 76–7

O

Oneness 101, 105, 128–9
ophanim 83

P

pagoda *105*
Paracelsus 102
paradise 8
Pardes 141
paths 56–79, 94, 141
patriarchs 141
pay 68
Penuel *see* Uriel
perceptions, restructuring 112–13
Persians 87, 90
Pesach 73
philosophers' stone 102
Pico (Giovanni Pico della Mirandola) 12, 137
Pillars 26–7, 28, 62, 106
Plato 21
Platonic Academy 12
Postel, Guillaume 137
prayer *128*, 129
prayer beads *129*
prophets 141
psychological consciousness 20
Purim 75
Pythagoras 95, 100

Q

quantum physics 61

R

Rachel 6
Rafael, archangel 85, *87*, 88, 141
Rebeccah 6, 141
Recanati, Menachem 137
reincarnation 93, 141
Renaissance 12
resh 64
Reuchlin, Johannes 12, 137
Rinzai 104
Rodin, François Auguste 48
Rokeach, Eliezer ben Yehuda 121, 135
Rosenroth, Knorr von 13
Rosh Hashanah 76

Rosicrucians 93
ruach 101, 141

S

Safed, Israel 136–7
Sagittarius 78
salt 102
Samael 42, 141
samech 70, 78
Sandalphon 84, 141
Sanhedrin 140
Sarah 6, 141
Satan 42, 87
Saturn 64, 65
Schachter–Shalomi, Zalman 139
scholars 130–1
Scholem, Gershom 139
science, paths and 61
Scorpio 77
Sefer ha-Bahir 24, 28, 71, 132, 133, 141
Sefer ha-Rimmon 26
Sefer Yetzirah 6, 19, 20, 28, 32, 35, 38, 54, 56, 60, 61, 62, 82, 94, 132, 133, 141
sefirah 141
sefirot 24, 32–55, 33
  correspondence to chakras 98–9
  paths 56–79, 94
self-control 51
self-isolation 118
sensory organs 69
serafim 82
Seven Doubles 62–9
sexuality 50–1
Shaarei Tzedek 63
Shabbat (Sabbath) 18, *40*, 52, 141
Shabbatai, Donolo 135
Shavuot 73
Shekhinah 49, 52, 65, 74, 136, 141
Shema 88
Shimon bar Yochai, Rabbi 133, 134
shin 58, 59
Simon the Just 28
Socrates 55
Solomon, King *36*, 133, 141
Solomon ibn Gabirol 135
Sophia *36*
Soto Zen 104–5
soul 93, 101, 118, 141

Spain 136
spirit 16
spiritual ascent 92–3
study 110
Sufism 100, 101, 141
sulphur 102
Sun 63, 64
  eclipse *12*
  superego 141
  synagogue 69
  synthesis 58, 100

T

Tai Chi *107*
Talmud 8, 86, 88, 133, 141
Tantric Yoga 103
Taoism 106–7
Tarfon, Rabbi 23, 127
Taurus 73
tav 64, 65
Temple of Solomon, plan 8
ten, power of 96
Ten Commandments 28–9, 96
tet 70, 76
Tetragrammaton 12, 32, 72, 96, 121, 141
thesis 58, 100
Thirty-Six 116
Three Mothers 58–9
Three Pillars 26–7, 28, 62, 106
Tiferet 22, 24, 26, 30, 32, 44–5, 52, 62–3, 64, 76, 78, 79, 83, 99, 141
tikkum 141
tikkun olam 17, 22, 101, 107, 141
Toledo *134*
Torah 8, 9, 21, 26, 34, 52, *55*, 73, 97, 133, 134–5, 141
Tree of Jesse *12*
Tree of Knowledge 26, 27, 54, 141
Tree of Life 6, *8*, *16*, 18, *18*, 22, 24–55, 98, 135, 141
  alchemy and *103*
  angels on *84*
  composition 26–7
  enneagram and 101, *101*
  paths 56–79, 94
  physical form and *92*
  Pillars 26–7, 28, 62, 106
  relevance today 30–1
  sefirot 24, 32–55, *33*
  Ten Commandments and 28–9, *29*

trigrams *106*
truth 97
Tsao Shan 104
Tung Shan 104
Twelve Elementals 70–9
Tzaddik 141
tzadi 70, 78, 79
Tzaphkiel *83*
Tzimtzum 17, 141

U

unification 29, 52, 54, 97, 101, 128–9, 141
Uriel, archangel 85, 86, 88, 141

V

vav 70, 72, 73
Venus 68, 69
virology 17
Vital, Rabbi Chaim 118, 137, 141

W

water 19, 61, 125
Watson, James 30
Wilkins, Maurice 30
Will, Divine 18–19, 116–17
wisdom 36
witchcraft 13

Y

Yesod 22, 24, 26, 30, 32, 50–1, 52, 64, 65, 76, 77, 99, 141
yetzer ha'ra 93, 113, 141
yetzer ha'tov 93, 113, 141
Yetzirah 14, 18, 19, 20–1, 141
YHVH 12, 32, 72, 96, 121, 141
yichud 52, 54, 97, 101, 128–9, 141
yin and yang 106, *107*, 141
yod 70, 76
Yom Kippur 76

Z

Zadkiel, archangel 141
Zaguto, Moses 128
zayin 4, 70
Zen 104–5, 141
zodiac 71, 108–9, 141
  human body and *108*
Zohar 12, 28, 37, 41, 82, 133, 134–5, *135*, 141

CREDITS

Quarto Publishing would like to acknowledge and thank the following for supplying pictures reproduced in this book:

(key: l left, r right, c center, t top, b bottom)

p19t The Art Archive, p23t Pictor, p31tl The Image Bank, p34br The Image Bank, p39r The Image Bank, p40br Trip, p41tr Trip, p42 The Bridgeman Art Library, p43r Pictor, p45r Pictor, p48bl The Art Archive, p55 Trip, p59tl Pictor, p62tr Pictor, p68tl NASA, p69t NASA, p69b Trip, p81 The Ronald Grant Archive, p83tr The Art Archive, p88bl The Ronald Grant Archive, p89t J-L Charmet, p91r National Library of Copenhagen, p100tr J-L Charmet, p101tl Trip, p105 tl Pictures Colour Library Ltd., p107t Image Bank, p118cr The Art Archive, p119bl Pictor, p124br J-L Charmet, p126br The Image Bank, p128br Pictor, p129t Trip, p132bl Pictor, p133t ffotograff, p134br Naomi Samuelson, p137t the Art Archive, p137br Clark/Clinch, p139tl J-L Charmet, p139bl J-L Charmet, p139br Israel Government Tourist Board.

Quarto Publishing would also like to thank the following for supplying props photographed in this book:

p2, 9 Finchley Reform Synagogue, London p73, 75, 77, 90, 97, and 109 The Great Frog, Carnaby Street, London.

p119 Maurice and Shirley Samuelson All other photographs and illustrations are the copyright of Quarto.

While every effort has been made to credit contributors, Quarto would like to apologize should there have been any omissions or errors.